UNNATURAL DEATH

Unnatural Death

Medicine's Descent from Healing to Killing

Richard Weikart

Seattle Discovery Institute Press 2024

Description

In this wide-ranging history of euthanasia and assisted suicide, historian Richard Weikart takes us from the ancient Jews, Greeks, and Romans to the contemporary scene—where the urge to help people kill themselves has intensified, even to the point of pushing the reluctant towards death. How did we reach this place? *Unnatural Death* answers this question by tracing a complex and fascinating history of ideas, attitudes, and legal wranglings stretching from Socrates to Peter Singer and beyond. Along the way Weikart shows diverse thinkers wrestling with the tension between the unalienable preciousness of human life, and the longing to escape suffering and despair. As the author demonstrates, the Judeo-Christian tradition encouraged a culture of life, but the secular Enlightenment and Darwinian materialism have tugged us in a different direction. In the book's final pages, Weikart considers where these currents are pulling us, and what can be done to reverse course.

Library Cataloging Data

Unnatural Death: Medicine's Descent from Healing to Killing
by Richard Weikart
Cover design by Tri Widyatmaka
208 pages, 6 x 9 inches
Library of Congress Control Number: 2024941110
ISBN: 978-1-63712-046-0 (paperback), 978-1-63712-048-4 (Kindle), 978-1-63712-047-7 (EPUB)
BISAC: MED050000 MEDICAL / Ethics
BISAC: LAW082000 LAW / Right to Die
BISAC: MED039000 MEDICAL / History

Publisher Information

Discovery Institute Press, 208 Columbia Street, Seattle, WA 98104
Internet: http://www.discoveryinstitutepress.com
Published in the United States of America on acid-free paper.
First Edition, August 2024

ADVANCE PRAISE

In all his writings, Richard Weikart tackles the most controversial issues, and in this book he takes on euthanasia and assisted suicide. The only way to stand effectively against a harmful social trend is to first understand where it came from and how it developed. We must identify the cause to apply an appropriate cure. That's why Weikart's careful historical analysis is so needed in our day.

—**Nancy Pearcey**, Professor and Scholar in Residence, Houston Christian University, author of several books, including *Total Truth* and *Love Thy Body*

Euthanasia and assisted suicide are gaining respectability with appalling speed, and Richard Weikart's superb new book, *Unnatural Death: Medicine's Descent from Healing to Killing*, is a vitally important reply to the organized disposal of unwanted people. As state-sanctioned killing of the sick and the handicapped and even the merely troubled becomes more and more acceptable in previously civilized nations such as Canada, the Netherlands, Switzerland, and the United States, Weikart shines a light on this methodical obsession with ending the lives of vulnerable people. Weikart wields the most potent weapon we have against the culture of death: he tells the truth about what is happening in dark corners. "Medical Assistance in Dying"—i.e., medicalized killing—is organized legal homicide. Weikart's book is revealing for readers who are unfamiliar with the history of euthanasia, a guidebook for activists working to protect innocent human life, and hopefully, a legal brief for prosecutors in a future Nuremberg-style trial of the sadists and medical professionals complicit in these crimes against humanity.

—**Michael Egnor**, Professor of Neurosurgery, Renaissance School of Medicine, Stony Brook University

The culture of death wrongly interprets the term compassion to mean "to get rid of" rather than its true meaning, "to suffer with." In *Unnatural Death* Dr. Richard Weikart uses his formidable skills of historical analysis to show that when it comes to euthanasia and assisted suicide, the proponents of materialism, secularism, and Darwinism "should not be allowed to twist and co-opt the idea of 'dying with dignity.'" Reaching back to antiquity and the imperative to "first do no harm" in the Hippocratic Oath (which was ignored by most Greek physicians and the Stoics of Rome), Weikart explains that with the sundowning of the pagan Greco-Roman culture and the ascent of the Judeo-Christian belief in the sacredness of life, euthanasia, suicide, and infanticide were strictly prohibited into Medieval times. He then documents how the rise of an idealized version of Greco-Roman cultural norms during the Renaissance and Enlightenment led to the progressive erosion of the Judeo-Christian ethic of "love your neighbor as yourself" and put us on a slippery slope to a culture of death. Weikart highlights three main factors at play in a society that normalizes euthanasia and assisted suicide: (1) intrinsic human inequality, (2) the duty to die, and (3) a loss of trust in the physician-patient relationship.

As a hospice and palliative care physician for over twenty years, I regularly care for terminally ill patients. Occasionally one of them expresses interest in euthanasia or assisted suicide; and I can say that, as Dr. Weikart expresses it, "sidestepping the hard work of providing care to the suffering" by "offering people an 'easy way' to end their lives" is tempting. Care for the suffering and terminally ill is intellectually and emotionally draining, never mind time-consuming. At such moments my lodestar is the knowledge that human life has intrinsic and unalienable value, and that it is the physician's sacred duty to care for life, not attack it. As Dr. Weikart persuasively argues, herein lies the moral and ethical difference between an authentically compassionate society and its mere caricature.

Happily, Dr. Weikart does not end on a hopeless note of inevitable decline into a culture of death, but instead offers a way off the slippery slope and onto a path to a culture of life. Ideas have consequences. If you want to know how we got here and what we must do to correct the situation, I strongly recommend you read this book.

—**Howard Glicksman**, hospice physician and co-author of
  Your Designed Body

In *Unnatural Death*, Professor Richard Weikart offers a readable and comprehensive history of euthanasia and assisted suicide from the time of the ancient Greeks, through the centuries, to the contemporary world in which doctors are legally allowed to administer lethal injections in several countries and can prescribe drug overdoses to terminally ill patients in ten US states. The modern euthanasia movement claims to be based on respect for autonomy and compassion. But Weikart effectively demonstrates that from its genesis in the pernicious eugenics movement, assisted suicide/euthanasia theory and practice are rooted in a deep and disturbing disdain for human equality, presenting a potent threat, not only to the terminally ill not offered suicide prevention if they ask to die, but also to people with disabilities, the elderly, and even the mentally ill as so-called right-to-die laws expand over time. As Weikart puts it so well, true compassion means that "we should never succumb to the temptation to think that some people's lives are so valueless that we should help them kill themselves." To do otherwise is to abandon those most in need of our support and love.

—**Wesley J. Smith**, Chairman, Discovery Institute Center on
  Human Exceptionalism, host of the Humanize podcast
  (www.humanize.today), and author of the award-winning
  Culture of Death: The Age of "Do Harm" Medicine

Richard Weikart's new book, *Unnatural Death*, is a first-rate piece of historical work on the history of euthanasia. The history is mostly a

dark one as he traces it from the Greco-Roman period through today. The connection with the modern euthanasia movement and eugenics is particularly helpful. I especially commend his final sections rebutting the pro-euthanasia argument from autonomy and defending the concern that euthanasia is a slippery slope. This book is essential reading for anyone with an interest in this important area of bioethics.
—**Scott B. Rae**, Dean of Faculty and Professor of Christian Ethics, Talbot School of Theology, Biola University

I highly recommend Richard Weikart's powerful, accessible, and important book on euthanasia and assisted suicide. This volume provides not only the relevant historical background to the whole discussion but also an insightful analysis of euthanasia's inconsistencies, hypocrisies, tyrannies, and blasphemies. Weikart offers a more consistent pathway—one that robustly affirms a culture of life with its emphasis on human dignity, essential equality, and true autonomy, which are rooted in a Creator who has made each of us in his image.
—**Paul Copan**, Pledger Family Chair of Philosophy and Ethics, Palm Beach Atlantic University (Florida), and co-author of *An Introduction to Biblical Ethics: Walking in the Way of Wisdom* (IVP Academic)

CONTENTS

INTRODUCTION

WHEN SEVENTEEN-YEAR-OLD JONI EARECKSON TADA TRAGICALLY broke her neck in a 1967 diving accident, she was understandably devastated by the shocking news that she would be paralyzed from the neck down for the rest of her life. During the long months she lay in the hospital and then in a rehabilitation center, she contemplated suicide and even pleaded with a friend to help her commit suicide.[1] If assisted suicide had been a legal option for her—as it is today in Canada, the Netherlands, and elsewhere for those suffering from incurable conditions—it seems likely she would have ended her life.

Now, fifty-seven years later, Joni rejoices that she is still alive and able to help others. Certainly she has faced many challenges and difficulties in her life, but she still insists that she has had a life filled with joy, meaning, and purpose. Indeed, it is astonishing to learn of her numerous achievements. For many years she has devoted her life to improving the lives of people with disabilities. In 1988 she was appointed to serve on the National Council on Disability, which reviewed legislation and government regulations that affect people with disabilities. She and her colleagues on the council drafted the Americans with Disabilities Act, one of the most important pieces of US legislation to improve the lives of people with disabilities.

She also founded Joni and Friends, an organization which sponsors retreats for children with disabilities and their families, distributes wheelchairs for free in impoverished countries, and sets up centers in poor areas to help people with disabilities access health care. She has inspired millions of people through a biography and film about her life, through her radio program, and through her speaking engagements. She also has recorded music and completed (holding a brush between her teeth) many lovely paintings. What a loss, both to herself and to the world, if she had killed herself in the depths of her despair right after her injury.

Joni addressed the problem of assisted suicide in her 1992 book, *When Is It Right to Die?: Suicide, Euthanasia, Suffering, Mercy.* In this work she vociferously rejected suicide, assisted or otherwise. She expressed thankfulness that assisted suicide was not legal when she was a depressed teenager laid up in the hospital. The love and care of other people often rescued her, she said, from the temptation to end her life.

When a new edition of her book was released in 2018, Joni noted in the preface that the situation had grown worse in the intervening twenty-six years. Now "it is no longer a matter of merely 'supporting' a person who has decided that his or her own life is not worth living," she writes. "No, we are witnesses to more instances where the 'right to die' has been given to a person with no say in the matter."

Some people, so the argument goes, are so disabled that they can't decide for themselves whether to live or die. In such cases, according to the euthanasia movement, a properly merciful society would help such individuals to end their suffering, which would simultaneously relieve loved ones and medical staff of the burden of caring for the disabled individual, freeing them to put their energies to better use elsewhere.

As Joni notes, this is not the same thing as assisted suicide. For clarity's sake, here are some generally accepted definitions:

- Assisted suicide: A physician or other person provides the means for the patient to kill himself.
- Voluntary euthanasia: The patient asks to be killed and someone else kills him.
- Nonvoluntary euthanasia: The patient is incompetent, unconscious, or otherwise unable to consent, and someone else kills him.

- Involuntary euthanasia: The patient is capable of giving or refusing consent, but is not asked; or the patient is killed against his will.

- Passive euthanasia: A physician or other person withholds or withdraws life-saving measures from someone with the intent of causing death; a refusal to act causes death. (Note the problematic broadness of this definition. Not all situations where life-prolonging measures are withheld or withdrawn constitute euthanasia; in medical settings most do not).[2]

When I use the term "euthanasia" in these pages I am referring to active forms of euthanasia, unless otherwise noted.

Until the past few decades, assisted suicide and euthanasia were illegal almost everywhere in the world. That's largely because the influence of the Judeo-Christian worldview was pervasive. Traditionally Christianity taught that humans are created in the image of God, thus imbuing humans with great value. Because of its stress on the value of human life, Christianity rejected not only murder, but also suicide, assisted suicide, and euthanasia. To be clear, the terms *assisted suicide* and *euthanasia* do not refer to administering painkillers even if that has the unintended effect of hastening death. Christians have consistently defended the view that easing pain is acceptable, even if an unintended side-effect is the hastening of the patient's demise.[3] Assisted suicide and euthanasia refer instead to the intentional ending of a person's life, usually by poisonous pills or a lethal injection.

Over the past few centuries, especially since the eighteenth-century Enlightenment, secularization has slowly eroded the Judeo-Christian sanctity-of-life ethic, as I document painstakingly in my book *The Death of Humanity: And the Case for Life*. As intellectuals and opinion leaders jettisoned the Christian religion, they also called into question many Christian values, including its prohibitions on suicide and euthanasia.

The increased acceptance of assisted suicide and euthanasia led to the Netherlands, Belgium, and Switzerland becoming the first countries in the modern West to legalize various forms of these acts. Some other countries have followed suit, so now euthanasia or assisted suicide is legal in Germany, Austria, Spain, and Canada, among other countries.[4] Additionally, Washington, DC, and ten states in the US, including California, have legalized assisted suicide. However, opposition to assisted suicide is still prevalent enough that in most countries it is still illegal, and many efforts to legalize assisted suicide and euthanasia in the US and in other countries fail each year.

How a secular worldview undermines the Judeo-Christian sanctity-of-life ethic and paves the way for assisted suicide and euthanasia is illustrated in Yuval Noah Harari's bestselling book *Sapiens: A Brief History of Humankind*. There Harari explicitly rejects the famous statement from the US Declaration of Independence, "We hold these truths to be self-evident, that all men are created equal, that they are endowed by their Creator with certain unalienable rights, that among these are life, liberty, and the pursuit of happiness." Harari counters this with what he considers a scientific worldview, arguing:

> According to the science of biology, people were not "created." They have evolved. And they certainly did not evolve to be "equal."... Evolution is based on difference, not equality....
>
> "Created equal" should therefore be translated into "evolved differently."... Just as people were never created, neither, according to the science of biology, is there a "Creator" who "endows" them with anything. There is only a blind evolutionary process, devoid of any purpose, leading to the birth of individuals.... Equally there are no such things as rights in biology.[5]

By denying human equality, human rights, and purpose and meaning in life, Harari opposes the foundation for valuing human life, thus opening the door to acceptance of assisted suicide and euthanasia.

Harari's view is, I believe, fundamentally misguided. Human life does have value, purpose, and meaning. Some may object to my stating this and point out that my Christian worldview leads me to this conclusion, a conclusion I am free to hold and which others, with a different worldview, need not embrace. For those not constrained by Christianity, why not adopt Harari's nihilistic view?

First of all, other religions of the world agree with Christianity that human life has value, purpose, and meaning. Further, even most secularists recognize that human life has intrinsic value. It seems to be an intuition built into almost all of us. As I have shown in my short work *Made in the Image of God: Why Human Dignity Argues for a Creator*, some of the staunchest secularist intellectuals, who overtly denied the value of human life, were unable to live or speak consistently with that viewpoint.[6] Somehow, deep down, they understood that human life has value and purpose, even if they vigorously denied it because of their worldview.

Another way we can see that the vast majority of us recognize that human life has value is by considering the suicide prevention measures we fund. If human life has no value or purpose, then no suicide is a tragedy, but is rather just another "ho, hum" event without any moral significance. It's just a random rearrangement of chemicals in the cosmos. We know better, and this should lead us to recognize that all human lives have value; so any suicide— including the forms of assisted suicide currently being legalized in many places—is tragic.

Finally, history attests that when a culture does not draw a firm line protecting human life, it inevitably progresses to ending lives for all manner of reasons—often against the will of the victims and their families. This should be as troubling to the secular person as to the religious.

The first and most extensive portion of this book will examine in detail the history of suicide, assisted suicide, and euthanasia in Western culture. Along the way I will engage arguments for and against euthanasia and assisted suicide, but I will turn to those arguments most fully in the final two chapters. There I will provide a thorough critique of euthanasia and assisted suicide, exploring one of the most powerful arguments against euthanasia and assisted suicide: the slippery slope argument. And no, slippery slope arguments are not *necessarily* fallacious. Some slopes really are slippery and perilous, and as I will show, this is one of them. Finally, I will contest one of the most persuasive arguments in favor of euthanasia and assisted suicide: the autonomy argument. This is the "my body, my choice" position that declares an individual right to assisted suicide.

My purpose throughout these pages is to demonstrate how we as a culture came to devalue human life, and as a corollary point the way forward to a healthier, more truly compassionate way of approaching suffering and death.

1. THE DEVALUATION OF LIFE IN CLASSICAL ANTIQUITY

IN 1982 IN MELBOURNE, AUSTRALIA, THE JOY THAT NICK VUJICIC'S parents felt at his birth turned to dismay when they saw him for the first time. His arms and legs were missing because of a rare disorder. Unprepared for this, his mother was so shocked that she refused to hold him. However, after quickly coming to terms with her emotions, she and her husband accepted him, loved him, and did everything they could to help him succeed in life. They could not have imagined how fulfilling and joyful his life would become. Today Vujicic is a famous motivational speaker, best-selling author, husband, father, and Christian evangelist, whose book, *Life without Limits*, encourages others to live life to the fullest.

According to his own testimony, Vujicic is living an extremely happy life, despite his disabilities. He explains:

> At first they [my parents] assumed that there was no hope and no future for someone like me, that I would never live a normal or productive life. Today, though, my life is beyond anything we could have imagined. Every day I hear from strangers via telephone, e-mail, text, and Twitter. They approach me in airports, hotels, and restaurants and hug me, telling me that I have touched their lives in some way. I am truly blessed. I am *ridiculously* happy.[1]

This illustrates a commonplace observation of those who work with people with disabilities: those without serious disabilities are often very poor judges of the positive possibilities for people with disabilities (or of their own potential happiness if they were to become disabled). It is presumptuous for people to assume that disability inevitably leads to unhappiness, especially when there are so many examples of happy and fulfilled people who are disabled. Unfortunately, some people even conclude that those with disabilities or serious illnesses are better off dead. Vujicic counters this attitude by stating that "life isn't always rosy, but it is always worth living."[2]

Vujicic's story would probably have turned out quite differently if he had been born in ancient Greece or Rome. In those societies infanticide was common, especially for infants with disabilities. Most likely he would have been denied that joyful and contagious "life without limits" that has been so inspiring to multitudes who have heard him or read his books. Fortunately for him, however, he was born to devout Christian parents in a society still heavily influenced by the Judeo-Christian moral tradition, which offers the weak and sick love and compassion, rather than death.

But that is changing. As the influence of Judeo-Christian morality wanes in Europe and the US, deeds such as suicide and euthanasia grow palatable, especially among the intellectual elites. In matters of life and death we are going backwards to a more brutal time.

Suicide and Infanticide in Greek Societies

In ancient Greek society, unaided suicide, physician-assisted suicide, and infanticide were not uncommon. This might seem surprising in light of the now-famous Hippocratic Oath, composed anonymously in Greece around 400 BCE. In the Hippocratic Oath physicians agreed never to harm patients, saying further, "neither will I administer a poison to anybody when asked to do so, nor will I suggest such a course."[3] Most people (including myself) construe this as a ban against physician-assisted suicide and euthanasia. However, some scholars argue (implausibly, in my view) that this was merely a prohibition against using their knowledge to help someone commit murder.[4]

Famous though the oath is today, however, in ancient Greece it seems to have represented a minority position among Greek physicians, many of whom did help sick people commit suicide.[5] Indeed, in the first 1,500 years of its existence, the Hippocratic Oath was almost unknown. It was rediscovered in medieval times, when it was adapted to Christian ideas, and it only became prominent as an oath for physicians in Europe and the US in the eighteenth century.[6] The Hippocratic prohibition against assisted suicide was thus not very influential in ancient Greek and Roman society.[7]

However, some Greek philosophers agreed with the Hippocratic prohibition against assisted suicide because they rejected any kind of suicide. Pythagoreans, followers of the sixth-century BCE philosopher Pythagoras, were among the earliest to condemn suicide categorically. They believed in body-soul dualism and reincarnation, and they argued that humans have an obligation toward God not to leave their bodies before the time ordained by God.[8]

According to Plato's account in *Phaedo*, Socrates, who lived about a century after Pythagoras, used the same reasoning to condemn suicide. Socrates stated, "Yet I too believe that the gods are our guardians, and that we are a possession of theirs." Thus, he continued, "a man should wait, and not take his own life until God summons him, as he is now summoning me."[9] As indicated by the last phrase, Socrates did not see his own drinking of poison as a violation of this principle, because his death was being forced on him by the governing authorities, not by his own will. (Many believe that views ascribed to Socrates in Plato's dialogues may be more the position of Plato than Socrates, but whether these ideas belonged to Socrates or Plato, they were influential among Greek intellectuals.)

In Plato's later work, *The Republic*, Socrates discussed the way physicians should interact with patients with incurable illnesses. Socrates suggested that physicians should refrain from treating people whose serious illnesses made them unproductive, unless the doctors could actually cure the patients and restore them to productivity. He asserted that it is not in the interest of the state for ill, unproductive people to continue living "good-for-nothing lives." He stated that "if a man was not able to live in the ordinary way he [the physician] had no business to cure him; for such a cure would have been of no use either to himself, or to the State."[10] Socrates's reasoning here places the interests of society above the individual's desires. However, it seems clear that here he was not advocating assisted suicide or active euthanasia, but rather letting the patient die. Thus (in Plato's telling) Socrates comes down against both suicide and assisted suicide.

Plato himself, however, intimated in one of his last works that he considered suicide under some circumstances permissible. To be sure, he still took a largely negative view of suicide, going so far as to call for posthumous punishment of those committing suicide. (He thought they should be buried alone without any honor.) Nonetheless, Plato allowed for three exceptions: 1) if the state required it (this covered Socrates's situation); 2) if the person was "under the compulsion of some painful and inevitable misfortune"; and 3) if the person would otherwise suffer intolerable shame.[11] These exceptions, especially the second one, seem very broad and would presumably excuse the suicide of a terminally ill person suffering pain.

Aristotle, Plato's student, condemned suicide in his *Nicomachean Ethics*. He argued that suicide committed an injustice against the state, because the person was abandoning his civic responsibilities. Further, he argued that committing suicide to escape from pain or unpleasantness was cowardly: "To die to escape from poverty or love or anything painful is not the mark of a brave man, but rather of a coward; for it is softness to fly from what is troublesome, and such a man endures death not because it is noble but to fly from evil."[12] Thus it seems clear that Aristotle would not have approved of suicide or assisted suicide for those suffering illness.

However, Aristotle, like many of his fellow Greeks, did approve of infanticide for babies with significant disabilities. In his book *Politics* he even advocated laws banning the raising of deformed children.[13]

Most infanticide in the Greco-Roman world occurred through "exposing" the baby, i.e., by abandoning the newborn infant outside. This usually resulted in death, either by wild animals, thirst, or malnutrition. In some cases the baby would be rescued and adopted, often to be raised as a slave. However, disabled infants were only rarely adopted, so the vast majority perished.

While exposing disabled infants was commonplace in Greek and Roman society, many historians are skeptical about the Roman author Plutarch's story about the Spartans taking their children to the city elders, who would decide if the children were fit to live. This is likely mythical, as there is no evidence to corroborate Plutarch's account, which was written centuries after the events.[14] However, Spartan parents, like many other Greek parents, probably did abandon disabled children to their death.

Stoicism and Suicide

Around 300 BCE, the Greek philosopher Zeno of Citium (not to be confused with the earlier Zeno of Elea, famous for Zeno's paradoxes) founded the Stoic school of philosophy, which later would influence Rome. The Stoics believed that at death a person's soul was reunited with the cosmic soul or God. Thus they did not fear death, even as they denied personal immortality.

Stoicism emphasized the suppressing of emotions and the elevation of reason. While they did not believe suicide was always justifiable, they considered it rational to choose death when one's health or living circumstances were intolerable. And indeed, it is reported that when Zeno was old he killed himself after sustaining a foot injury.[15] Zeno's successor, Cleanthes, is likewise said to have committed suicide, in his case by voluntary starvation.[16]

A later Stoic philosopher, Chrysippus, listed five reasons justifying suicide: 1) if a pressing matter dictates it (such as an oracle telling one to kill oneself to save a city); 2) to keep from having to perform shameful things dictated by tyrants; 3) to escape serious illness; 4) to avoid poverty; and 5) if one became demented.[17]

Romans Embrace Suicide and Infanticide

Stoicism became a very popular philosophy among the Romans. The first-century Roman Stoic philosopher Seneca denied that anyone had an obligation to continue living, arguing that one should rationally choose the moment of one's demise. He wrote, "Accordingly, the wise man will live as long as he ought, not as long as he can.... He always reflects concerning the quality, and not the quantity, of his life."[18]

Seneca thus saw suicide as a rational choice in some situations, as, for instance, to escape suffering in seemingly hopeless circumstances. "In whatever direction you may turn your eyes, there lies the means to end your woes," he wrote. "See that precipice? Down that is the way to liberty. See you that sea, that river, that well? There sits liberty—at the bottom."[19] Elsewhere, he elaborated thus:

> If one death is accompanied by torture, and the other is simple and easy, why not snatch the latter? Just as I shall select my ship when I am about to go on a voyage or my house when I propose to take a residence, so I shall choose my death when I am about to depart from life.... There is no occasion when the soul should be humoured more than at the moment of death. Let the soul depart as it feels itself impelled to go; whether it seeks the sword, or the halter, or some draught that attacks the veins, let it proceed and burst the bonds of its slavery. Every man ought to make his life acceptable to others besides himself, but his death to himself alone. The best form of death is the one we like....
>
> You can find men who have gone so far as to profess wisdom and yet maintain that one should not offer violence to one's own life, and hold it accursed for a man to be the means of his own destruction; we should wait, say they, for the end decreed by nature. But one who says this does not see that he is shutting off the path to freedom.... Must I await the cruelty either of disease or of man, when I can depart through the midst of torture, and shake off my troubles?[20]

Seneca thus approved of suicide, as long as it was rationally considered rather than prompted by passion. When faced with the threat of execution by Emperor Nero at age sixty-eight, Seneca ended his life by slitting his wrists and then taking poison.

Influenced by Stoic thought, many other prominent Romans committed suicide as well, including Cato the Younger, who killed himself rather than submit to Julius Caesar. Roman accounts generally lauded his suicide as gallant and heroic.

Stoics were not the only ones justifying suicide in Roman society. Epicureans also regarded suicide as acceptable. Epicureans believed that the goal of life was the pursuit of pleasure, and this philosophy was very popular among ancient Romans.

Lucretius, a first-century-BCE Epicurean philosopher, denied the existence of anything non-material, explaining that in his view, "Death, then, is nothing to us, no concern / Once we grant that the soul will also die."[21] Lucretius did not spell out the implications of this for suicide, but it seems clear that the Epicurean philosophy provided no reason to oppose suicide.

Infanticide was likewise acceptable to Romans. Seneca wrote:

> We knock mad dogs on the head, we slaughter fierce and savage bulls, and we doom scabby sheep to the knife, lest they should infect our flocks: we destroy monstrous births, and we also drown our children if they are born weakly or unnaturally formed; to separate what is useless from what is sound is an act, not of anger, but of reason.[22]

Seneca and other Stoics, in other words, thought that killing infants who had disabilities was simply the reasonable thing to do, no different from killing mad dogs or scabby sheep.

And infanticide was not limited to children with disabilities. Fathers in the Roman empire (with whom the decision rested) might choose to kill a child because of the family's economic situation, or because the child was a girl, or because of omens or the positions of the stars.[23]

They had little concern for the sanctity or value of human life.

The Hebrews Reject Suicide

Not everyone in antiquity devalued life. The ancient Hebrews—also known as Israelites or Jews—took a contrary stance.[24]

The Hebrew Bible (the Christian "Old Testament") did not explicitly forbid suicide, but its teachings were incompatible with suicide. It depicted humans as responsible to a loving God, who created people in his image. This provided a foundation for valuing human life as sacred. Further, some (including the extremely influential church leader Augustine) have argued that when the Ten Commandments forbid murder, this includes suicide because suicide can be construed as "self-murder." (Interestingly, this was the English term for it before the word "suicide" was coined in the seventeenth century.)

The few accounts of suicides in the Hebrew Bible do not convey approval of the act, but generally present suicide or assisted suicide as the bad end of people who generally made bad choices. For instance, Abimelech murdered his seventy brothers in order to secure his position, hired "reckless scoundrels" as his henchmen, and wreaked bloody havoc on various towns. Then,

> Abimelech went to Thebez, and he encamped against Thebez and took it. But there was a strong tower in the city, and all the men and women—all the people of the city—fled there and shut themselves in; then they went up to the top of the tower. So Abimelech came as far as the tower and fought against it; and he drew near the door of the tower to burn it with fire. But a certain woman dropped an upper millstone on Abimelech's head and crushed his skull. Then he called quickly to the young man, his armor-bearer, and said to him, "Draw your sword and kill me, lest men say of me, 'A woman killed him.'" So his young man thrust him through, and he died. And when the men of Israel saw that Abimelech was dead, they departed, every man to his place.
>
> Thus God repaid the wickedness of Abimelech, which he had done to his father by killing his seventy brothers. And all the evil of the men of Shechem God returned on their own heads, and on them came the curse of Jotham the son of Jerubbaal.[25]

Interestingly, no biblical character committed suicide in response to an illness. Indeed, when righteous Job suffered from an excruciating illness after experiencing unparalleled tragedy (the death of his children and loss of his wealth), his wife encouraged him to "curse God and die." But Job replied, "You speak as one of the foolish women speaks. Shall we indeed accept good from God, and shall we not accept adversity?"[26]

The story of Job provides a poignant example of patience in the face of pain and suffering, which God rewarded in the end. The New Testament writer James praised Job thus: "My brethren, take the prophets, who spoke in the name of the Lord, as an example of suffering and patience. Indeed we count them blessed who endure. You have heard of the perseverance of Job and seen the end intended by the Lord—that the Lord is very compassionate and merciful."[27] One of the lessons from Job's experiences, then, is that we should endure suffering rather than escape it through suicide.

Indeed, Judaism, both before and after the rise of Christianity, has generally condemned suicide as immoral. There are exceptions, including the mass suicide of 960 Jews at Masada[28] around 73 CE—though it should be noted that a distinction was drawn between suicide under intense mental or physical strain (such as when enemies are at the gates) and suicide in less dire situations.[29] The first-century writer Josephus, for instance, referred to this distinction when he was trapped with forty others facing Roman capture. He argued that because the Romans only intended to capture them, not kill them, they should not kill themselves:

> It is a brave thing to die in war; but so that it be according to the law of war, by the hand of conquerors. If, therefore, I avoid death from the sword of the Romans, I am truly worthy to be killed by my own sword, and my own hand; but if they admit of mercy, and would spare their enemy, how much more ought we to have mercy upon ourselves, and to spare ourselves?[30]

However, Josephus then expanded his argument to prohibit even suicide in the face of impending death:

> What are we afraid of, when we will not go up to the Romans? Is it death? If so, what we are afraid of, when we but suspect our enemies will inflict it on us, shall we inflict it on ourselves for certain? But it may be said we must be slaves. And are we then in a clear state of liberty at present? It may also be said that it is a manly act for one to kill himself. No, certainly, but a most unmanly one; as

I should esteem that pilot to be an arrant coward, who, out of fear of a storm, should sink his ship of his own accord.[31]

And, finally, Josephus argued that our lives are a gift from God:

Now self-murder is a crime most remote from the common nature of all animals, and an instance of impiety against God our Creator; nor indeed is there any animal that dies by its own contrivance, or by its own means, for the desire of life is a law engraven in them all; on which account we deem those that openly take it away from us to be our enemies, and those that do it by treachery are punished for so doing. And do not you think that God is very angry when a man does injury to what he hath bestowed on him? For from him it is that we have received our being, and we ought to leave it to his disposal to take that being away from us.[32]

Thus Josephus came down firmly against suicide, even in situations where the alternative is capture and death.[33] The Talmud, which aside from the Bible is the most influential set of Jewish religious writings, firmly condemns both suicide and assisted suicide, but includes concessions for extenuating circumstances.[34] Most branches of Judaism have continued to reject suicide throughout the centuries, though this may be loosening some in the last few decades.[35]

The ancient Jews also rejected infanticide. A Roman historian named Tacitus noted that the Jews "take thought to increase their numbers," and regard it as a crime to kill even "late-born" children, i.e., children born after the father's will is made out and no more children in the family are desired.[36]

Josephus confirmed Tacitus's account, writing that Jewish law "enjoins us to bring up all our offspring, and forbids women to cause abortion of what is begotten, or to destroy it afterward; and if any woman appears to have so done, she will be a murderer of her child, by destroying a living creature, and diminishing humankind."[37]

Christianity Rejects Suicide

Building on their Jewish roots (Jesus and his apostles were Jews), Christians have had a dim view of suicide from the beginning.[38] The only suicide recorded in the New Testament is that of Judas, the man who betrayed Jesus to his enemies; here again suicide is connected with immorality.[39] And while there is no out-and-out prohibition on suicide in the New Testament, there are certainly many teachings that hint at the immorality of suicide. For instance, Paul wrote to the Corinthians that their bodies were temples of the Holy Spirit. He adjured them, "If anyone defiles the temple of God, God will destroy him. For the temple of God is holy, which temple you are." He also argued that our bodies are not our own, but belong to God, a point that Socrates had used earlier as an argument against suicide.[40] And Paul wrote to the Ephesians that "no one ever hated his own flesh, but nourishes and cherishes it," suggesting that harming oneself is not a natural impulse.[41]

Further, the New Testament often encourages Christians to endure suffering and tribulations patiently, experiences God can use to purify people's hearts. This implies that suicide is not a righteous response to suffering, because—as the writer of Hebrews puts it—one would be illegitimately escaping from God's beneficial but painful process of chastisement. "If you endure chastening," Hebrews tells us, "God deals with you as with sons; for what son is there whom a father does not chasten?"[42]

Christians also were instructed to confront sickness by praying for divine healing.[43] The New Testament contains many accounts of divine healing, not only during Jesus's ministry, but also by the apostles later. The hope of divine healing could be a powerful incentive not to commit suicide. And even when healing was not given—as it was not given to the apostle Paul—the focus remained on trusting God, not on taking matters into one's own hands.[44]

The New Testament encourages Christians not only to endure suffering, but even to rejoice in the face of it. Jesus stated, "In the world you will have tribulation; but be of good cheer, I have overcome the world."[45]

Like suicide, infanticide is not specifically mentioned in the New Testament, but clearly infanticide is included in the sin of murder, which is mentioned quite frequently. Moreover, Jesus instructed his disciples to accept little children and warned them severely against causing any sort of harm to children. He stated, "Take heed that you do not despise one of these little ones, for I say to you that in heaven their angels always see the face of my Father who is in heaven.... it is not the will of your Father who is in heaven that one of these little ones should perish."[46]

Would this include children with disabilities? Clearly it would, because Jesus consistently urged his disciples to help the weak and the sick. He taught, "But when you give a feast, invite the poor, the maimed, the lame, the blind. And you will be blessed, because they cannot repay you."[47] Killing disabled infants would fly in the face of everything Jesus taught about the importance of loving the meek and weak members of society.

Suicide was not mentioned all that frequently in extra-biblical literature of the early church, but twelve of the early church fathers condemned it.[48] The second-century Christian leader Justin Martyr, for example, countered the suggestion (by non-Christians) that Christians should escape persecution by committing suicide. He explained in his *Second Apology* that suicide would be an act opposing God's will, because God created us for a purpose, and we should not hinder his purposes.[49]

No early Christian leader ever mentioned in their writings examples of suicide to escape illness. However, by the fourth century, some Christian leaders, including Ambrose and Jerome, did allow for an exception to the general prohibition against suicide: women facing rape could escape by killing themselves.[50] In his early fourth-century book *Church History*, Eusebius related with apparent approval the story of three Christian women who, after being captured by Roman soldiers, flung themselves into a river and perished to avoid further persecution and mistreatment, especially rape.[51]

Early Christian writers condemned infanticide. The earliest Christian document to explicitly condemn infanticide was the *Didache*, an anonymous early second-century text that stated, "Do not murder a child by abortion, nor kill it at birth."[52] Other early Christian leaders opposed infanticide, including Justin Martyr and Tertullian.[53]

Moreover, no ancient sources that we know about mention Christians exposing their children.[54] Influenced by Christianity, Emperor Valentinian I banned infanticide in 374.[55]

Augustine discussed suicide extensively in *City of God* (circa 413–418), and his condemnation of suicide became the official teaching of the Christian churches for centuries thereafter. Augustine was especially concerned to refute the notion that chaste Christian virgins were justified in committing suicide to escape rape. He asserted that suicide was categorically wrong, since the command "thou shalt not kill" did not exclude killing oneself. In the case of rape, he maintained that the victims were still pure and holy—rape defiled the rapist, not the victim—so they had no cause to kill themselves to avoid sin.

In the case of Christians who thought they should kill themselves to avoid future sin, he remonstrated that this would be foolish, because it would mean perpetrating a great sin to try to avoid a possible future sin (and giving oneself no opportunity to repent of that sin). Augustine also rejected suicide for the sake of escaping suffering or persecution, because he believed it was better to endure suffering courageously.[56] He summed up his position thus:

> But this we affirm, this we maintain, this we every way pronounce to be right, that no man ought to inflict on himself voluntary death, for this is to escape the ills of time by plunging into those of eternity; that no man ought to do so on account of another man's sins, for this were to escape a guilt which could not pollute him, by incurring great guilt of his own; that no man ought to do so on account of his own past sins, for he has all the more need of this life that these sins may be healed by repentance; that no man should put an end to this life to obtain that better life we look for after death, for those who die by their own hand have no better life after death.[57]

Augustine only admitted one exception to the prohibition against suicide: if God commanded one to do so. He assumed that Samson had received such an order justifying his behavior (though Scripture does not indicate that God told him to do it, so it is not clear why Augustine thought this was the case).

Beyond Antiquity

The Roman Empire lost much of its power by 476, thus ending the era of classical antiquity. The Judeo-Christian tradition continued, carrying with it a firm prohibition against suicide, euthanasia, and infanticide. Notably, the most famous and influential among the medieval theologians, Thomas Aquinas, agreed wholeheartedly with Augustine about suicide (as did all other medieval theologians). He devoted a brief section of his magisterial *Summa Theologica* to the question: "Whether it is lawful to kill oneself?" In addition to an appeal to the divine command "thou shalt not kill," Aquinas provided three other reasons why suicide is wrong. "First," he explained, "because everything naturally loves itself... Wherefore suicide is contrary to the inclination of nature and to charity whereby every man should love himself." Second, he cited Aristotle's position that every person belongs to the community and thus anyone committing suicide sins against the community. Third, he argued that "life is God's gift to man, and is subject to His power, Who kills and makes to live. Hence whoever takes his own life, sins against God." Aquinas agreed with Augustine that only God's direct command to take one's life would provide justification for such an act.[58]

Meanwhile, the Catholic Church's rejection of suicide led it to stress the danger of hell-fire for a person committing suicide. To underscore this point, if a person committed suicide, the Catholic Church would not allow that person's body to be buried in hallowed ground with last rites.

Reflecting this negativity toward suicide, many medieval European monarchs and lawmakers imposed civil penalties on suicide. Some of these penalties, such as desecrating the corpse, were posthumous punishment for the person who committed suicide. Other measures, such as forfeiture of the dead person's estate, punished a person's heirs, rather than the perpetrator. It is not clear how effective these measures were as deterrents, especially since they were often evaded, sometimes by claiming the person who committed suicide was insane. However, the laws did reflect a staunch rejection of suicide as immoral.[59]

Conclusion

From ancient times the Judeo-Christian belief in the sacredness of life pushed back against the more cavalier attitude of the Greeks and Romans. And, of course, Judaism and Christianity continued while the empires of Greece and Rome fell.

However, as we shall see in the next chapter, the empires of ancient Greece and Rome, though gone, were not forgotten. Their ideas would resurface and begin anew the debate about choosing death.

2. RENAISSANCE
AND ENLIGHTENMENT

AFTER MANY CENTURIES DURING WHICH THE JUDEO-CHRISTIAN
ethos prevailed, attitudes towards suicide began to change during the fourteenth to sixteenth centuries. This was the Renaissance, a movement in Europe characterized by a desire to restore ("rebirth," hence "renaissance") ancient Greco-Roman culture—or, rather, an idealized version of it. In this period many Europeans admired the Stoics and began reading the ancient Greek and Roman classics, some of which glorified suicide. This elevation of Greek and Roman culture began to effect a very gradual change in attitudes toward suicide.

The change was slowed by the ongoing influence of Christianity. Throughout the Renaissance the Catholic Church continued its staunch opposition to suicide, and the newly emerging Protestant churches in the sixteenth century were just as vehement. The Protestant leader Martin Luther (1483–1546) regarded suicide as evil, as the work of Satan. However, he stated, "I don't share the opinion that suicides are certainly to be damned. My reason is that they do not wish to kill themselves but are overcome by the power of the devil."[1]

In his sermons on Job, the leading Reformed theologian John Calvin (1509–1564) claimed that while Christians should desire death, they should do so because they long to escape from sin and enter into perfection, not because they are sick or suffering (as Job was). Calvin declared, "Thus we see that the children of God must bear their adversities patiently, although God chastise them roughly for a time." Because of this, he insisted, Christians should wait on God's timing and not end their lives by their own decision.[2]

Death in Utopia

One of the more controversial pieces of sixteenth-century literature to broach the subject of suicide was Thomas More's *Utopia* (1516). Literary scholars and historians disagree sharply over More's meaning, in part because many aspects of his fictional island Utopia do not mesh well with his commitment to Roman Catholicism. More was, after all, known for rooting out heresy; and his refusal to sanction both the annulment of Henry VIII's marriage to Catherine of Aragon, and Henry's claim to have authority over the church, resulted in his execution. He seems an unlikely one, then, to take a stance directly opposed to church doctrine.

Thus while some insist that in *Utopia* More was portraying an ideal society to which we should aspire, others interpret his utopian society as a parody, a warning against the folly and dangers of utopianism. I side with the view that More's society is dystopian. Even setting aside what is known about the author, in the fictional world so many characteristics of the society seem either off-putting—such as reintroducing slavery and even enslaving people who travel without the government's permission—or bizarre, such as Utopia's citizens listening to lectures before daybreak. Thus I take his description of suicide in Utopia not as a radical prescription for it, but as a warning against it.[3]

In any case, in the society More described, dying patients who are suffering pain are not only allowed, but even encouraged, to commit suicide to escape their sorrow. According to More, in Utopia,

> when any is taken with a torturing and lingering pain, so that there is no hope either of recovery or ease, the priests and magistrates come and exhort them, that, since they are now unable to go on with the business of life, are become a burden to themselves and to all about them, and they have really out-lived themselves, they should no longer nourish such a rooted distemper, but choose rather to die since they cannot live but in much misery; being assured

that if they thus deliver themselves from torture, or are willing that others should do it, they shall be happy after death: since, by their acting thus, they lose none of the pleasures, but only the troubles of life, they think they behave not only reasonably but in a manner consistent with religion and piety; because they follow the advice given them by their priests, who are the expounders of the will of God.[4]

More certainly understood the psychology of the issue, mentioning many of the same reasons that advocates today proffer in support of assisted suicide. Note, however, that More's society was not characterized by individual freedom, but rather by paternalistic authoritarianism with just about everything regulated. The governing authorities decided whether each suicide was allowed, just as they decided everyone's bedtime and the number of children each family could have.

While today's assisted suicide proponents like to claim More as one of their own based on this passage from *Utopia*, they ignore not only his personal history and the dystopian nature of his text, but also his other writings, where he explicitly rejected suicide. In his 1522 work, *The Four Last Things*, More made it clear that suicide was immoral. Then, in 1534, while he was imprisoned in the Tower, More penned *A Dialogue of Comfort against Tribulation*, which contains an extensive passage on suicide. In it he explicitly relied on Augustine's arguments and argued vociferously that suicide is sinful, and that one is not permitted to resort to suicide to escape from tribulation and suffering.[5]

Recalling Greece and Rome

One of the earliest major European thinkers who discussed suicide with some degree of approval was Michel de Montaigne, the sixteenth-century French writer known for his religious skepticism. Montaigne, understanding how radical it would be to defend suicide overtly, instead described—sometimes rather sympathetically—various suicides from ancient Greece and Rome. He provided reasons for committing suicide and reasons against it. Overall, however, it seems that he considered suicide acceptable, and he stated, "Pain and the fear of a worse death seem to me the most excusable incitements" to suicide.[6] In 1601 one of Montaigne's friends, the renegade Catholic priest Pierre Charon, defended suicide more forthrightly than Montaigne, and his book was soon placed on the Catholic Church's Index of Forbidden Books.[7]

Dramatizing Suicide

Sometime around 1570 suicide became a more prominent theme in European literature, especially in drama. Literature itself of course had exploded after the invention of the printing press, whose use spread throughout Europe by 1500 or so. As more and more people wrote, more and more people included suicide in their tales. Between 1580 and 1620 English dramatists portrayed some two hundred suicides in one hundred plays. While conceding that most of the plays do not discuss the propriety of suicide, Georges Minois notes that many of the suicides in these plays are depicted "in a favorable light as an admirable act."[8]

Shakespeare's work contains quite a few suicides.[9] Some of his plays were set in ancient Rome, and those plays reflect with historical accuracy the Roman culture's acceptance of suicide. For instance, in *Julius Caesar,* Cassius and Brutus fall on their swords after a humiliating defeat. *Othello*, set in Italy though not in ancient times, portrays the main character's suicide as self-execution after he murders his wife in a fit of jealousy and then discovers that she was innocent and that he had been misled into believing she had betrayed him.

In plays set elsewhere (Denmark, Scotland, etc.) Shakespeare portrayed suicide in various ways, including as the result of a guilty conscience (the off-stage suicide of Lady Macbeth, whose hands were metaphorically and literally stained with the blood); as the byproduct of insanity (Ophelia, likely driven mad after her beloved inadvertently slew her father, accidentally falls into water and then doesn't take action to save herself from drowning); and as a tragic teenage overreaction (Romeo and Juliet). In none of these examples is the suicide presented in a positive light.

Shakespeare's play *Hamlet* explicitly discusses the moral quandary surrounding the act of suicide. In Shakespeare's best-known soliloquy, Hamlet says:

To be or not to be—that is the question:
Whether 'tis nobler in the mind to suffer
The slings and arrows of outrageous fortune,
Or to take arms against a sea of troubles
And, by opposing, end them.

Hamlet never really answers the question, though he does suggest that the fear of death and what comes after death hinders most people from taking their own lives: "For in that sleep of death what dreams may come,/ When we have shuffled off this mortal coil,/ Must give us pause."[10]

In the same play, characters discuss the temporal and eternal fate of a presumed suicide. Gravediggers comment that Ophelia is only buried in consecrated ground because her family is influential; the priest refuses to perform a full burial ceremony because "to do more would profane the service of the dead"; and Laertes strongly objects to these denigrations, telling the priest, "A ministering angel shall my sister be, when thou liest howling."[11] These elements read less as an approval of suicide and more as the impassioned protest of a loving brother against the priest's judgmental handling of a difficult case, one in which the deceased had likely been out of her head with grief.[12]

Thus Shakespeare sometimes depicted suicide as the final bad choice in a life of bad choices, and sometimes he depicted it with pity and some measure of understanding. The question of how to express compassion without conveying approval—or worse, encouraging suicide—is, of course, a difficult one.

And Then There Was Donne

The famous clergyman and writer John Donne, Shakespeare's contemporary, was one of the earliest influential Europeans to overtly contradict Augustine's position on suicide. Sometime around 1608 he wrote a treatise, *Biathanatos*,[13] which argued that suicide was not necessarily sinful. Donne—who suffered from depression, then known as "melancholy"—admitted that he often had a "sickly inclination" toward suicide and urged a more charitable attitude towards those who succumb.[14] This was controversial enough; but Donne created further scandal by implying that the death of Jesus was a suicide, interpreting Jesus's crucifixion this way because Jesus had said he was laying down his life voluntarily. (Most Christians—then and today—consider Donne's characterization of Christ's death not only wrong, but bizarre).

Because Donne's position was so controversial, he did not publish *Biathanatos* during his lifetime, but only passed the manuscript along to close friends to read. His son later published it posthumously in 1646 or 1647. Donne's openness to suicide was not shared by most of his contemporaries, and many English clergymen, horrified by Donne's position, wrote responses rejecting suicide.

The Church Holds the Line

Thirty years later, *Pilgrim's Progress* (1678) illustrated Protestants' continued rejection of suicide. Written by the Baptist pastor John Bunyan, the work was probably the best-selling English book of the seventeenth century (aside from the Bible). In it, when the pilgrim named Christian and his companion Hopeful wander off the right path and end up in the prison of Giant Despair, the giant inflicts torment on them and counsels them to commit suicide. Christian seems tempted to end his life, telling Hopeful, "The life that we now live is miserable. For my part, I know not whether is best, to live thus, or to die out of hand." However, Hopeful replies:

> Indeed, our present condition is dreadful, and death would be far more welcome to me than thus for ever to abide; but yet, let us consider, the Lord of the country to which we are going hath said, Thou shalt do no murder: no, not to another man's person; much more, then, are we forbidden to take his counsel to kill ourselves. Besides, he that kills another, can but commit murder upon his body; but for one to kill himself, is to kill body and soul at once. And, moreover, my brother, thou talkest of ease in the grave; but

hast thou forgotten the hell, whither for certain the murderers go? For "no murderer hath eternal life."

True to his name, Hopeful then offers hope to his friend that God will not forsake them. He suggests they may soon escape the clutches of the giant, which indeed they do. Clearly Bunyan's tale was intended to provide encouragement and hope to those contemplating suicide so that they would not kill themselves.[15]

This was typical. In the mid-seventeenth century, European societies almost universally condemned suicide as immoral, as had been the consensus for many centuries. Despite a couple of renegade clergymen, such as Donne, the Christian churches were solidly arrayed against the idea.

But as we have seen, under the influence of the Renaissance's admiration for Greco-Roman culture, literature and drama began to explore suicide and its causes more frequently. It was at this time that the new English word "suicide" was introduced to replace the term "self-murder." What would start as a small crack in the anti-suicide bulwark would expand considerably in the ensuing Enlightenment period, where the propriety of suicide became a subject of considerable discussion.

Deism and Death

In a sensational and gruesome murder and double suicide in 1732, the London bookbinder Richard Smith and his wife Bridget shot their infant in the head and then hanged themselves. They were despondent because they had amassed debts and foresaw nothing but poverty and misery in their future. Their horrific deed captured considerable public attention, and Voltaire, relating their story years later, averred, "I do not know any act of cold-blooded horror so striking as this."[16]

However, Voltaire also mentioned the peculiar nature of their suicide note, which aroused dismay and indignation in some quarters. In their note the Smiths justified their suicidal behavior by appealing to a deistic worldview, i.e., the idea that God had created the world, but then did not interact with it in any meaningful way.

Deism was becoming increasingly popular among intellectuals in Europe during the so-called "Enlightenment" of the late seventeenth and eighteenth centuries, and it certainly made suicide seem permissible in a way that more traditional Christian views did not. (If God is distant and impersonal, perhaps he does not care whether we live or die.) Likewise the rise in religious skepticism (often called "free-thinking" at that time) eliminated religious qualms about suicide.[17]

The Smith suicides—though the most sensational—were not the first in England inspired or influenced by Enlightenment thought. Just four years earlier Robert Jennens, an Oxford graduate whose brother later became the librettist for Handel's *Messiah*, committed suicide. His suicide was apparently influenced by the deistic ideas of an Oxford classmate and friend, Nicholas Stevens.[18]

The religious sceptic Thomas Creech, an Oxford scholar who translated the works of the Roman philosopher Lucretius, hanged himself in 1700. Since Lucretius's philosophy was atheistic and materialistic, this touched off speculation that Creech's irreligious philosophy motivated him to commit suicide.[19] In 1693 one of the leading English deists of the late seventeenth century, Charles Blount, committed suicide at age thirty-nine, and critics considered it corroboration of the evils of his deistic worldview.

Of course, it would be simplistic to say that "free-thinking" deism led inevitably to an approval of suicide. In 1712, when a free-thinking lawyer William Blencowe shot himself, his friend Matthew Tindal, a leading English deist, was blamed for his suicide, because many thought Tindal's philosophy had contributed to it. Tindal, however, considered suicide immoral.[20]

While it is difficult to ascertain the degree to which deism or skepticism contributed to any one suicide, it is clear that the rate of suicides rose significantly in late seventeenth-century and early eighteenth-century England. The increase began with a sharp rise in 1683, followed by a continuing upsurge over the next several decades, including a sharp spike in 1700. One scholar who has examined the history of the English debate over suicide in the late seventeenth and early eighteenth centuries, S. E. Sprott, argues that the libertine attitudes of Enlightenment thinkers, which were gaining currency in late seventeenth-century England, fueled the rise of suicides after 1683 (even though some leading deists rejected suicide). He calls the period 1683–1720 the libertine era of suicide, because some (especially among the intellectual elites) were spurning traditional Christian morality and justifying suicide. He explains, "The milieu of suicide [in late seventeenth- and early eighteenth-century England] must be sought less in any particular system than in a new cultural and social ideal of behavior based on a combination of Epicurean values and libertine principles of thinking."[21] Epicureanism lent support for suicide by exalting pleasure (and the avoidance of pain) above any other moral consideration.

Suicide rates continued to escalate in the period 1720 to 1750, which Sprott calls the rationalist era of suicide. During this era, more people appealed to reason to justify their suicides, and often these justifications were based on an atheistic worldview, rather than a deistic one. In their study of the history of suicide in early modern England, historians Michael MacDonald and Terence Murphy likewise argue that Enlightenment ideas—especially deism and atheism—loosened attitudes against suicide.[22]

In 1732, shortly before the Smiths' infamous suicides, Alberto Radicati di Passerano published *A Philosophical Dissertation upon Death*, a book dedicated to defending suicide.[23] Radicati was an aristocrat from Piedmont (in what is now northern Italy) who embraced Enlightenment ideas. One of the primary points of the book, he wrote, was to prove that suicide is "at all Times a laudable Action; and at no Times blameable; natural, and not contrary to *Nature*."[24] Radicati's book appeared in London, where he had moved to escape religious persecution from Piedmontese authorities. We do not know if the Smiths read Radicati's work, but the ideas they espoused bore some similarity to his. Critics of Radicati certainly considered the Smiths' deeds a powerful demonstration of the perils of Enlightenment thought.

In his book Radicati laid the foundation for his view of death by first explaining his view of nature and existence, which seems to be derived largely from Baruch Spinoza's influential philosophy. Spinoza argued for a pantheistic worldview, i.e., the position that God and nature are identical, using appeals to reason and logic. Radicati asserted that matter and motion are eternal, and he ascribed to them traits of divinity. He stated, "This *Matter*, modified by *Motion* into an infinite Number of various Forms, is that which I call NATURE. Of this the Qualities and Attributes are, *Power, Wisdom,* and *Perfection*, all which she possesses in the highest Degree." Like Spinoza, he insisted that natural laws are deterministic, so there is no divine will that can contravene natural laws. Nature is all that exists. On this basis, Radicati defined life as simply a "modification of matter" and death as merely the "dissolution of the Corporeal Parts" of an organism. He clearly did not believe humans had non-physical souls.[25]

After setting forth this pantheistic vision of reality, Radicati turned his attention to morality. He denied that morals are innate, and he provided numerous examples of the way that moral standards vary from one culture to another. Despite this moral relativism, he proposed two criteria to determine the morality of human behavior. The first, inspired by the resurgence of Epicurean philosophy in the Enlightenment, was whether the behavior is conducive to public happiness. The second, in harmony with his Spinozism, was whether the behavior was in conformity with nature. In one sense, Radicati thought all human behavior was consistent with nature, because he insisted on determinism in human affairs, stating, "Besides, if we examine into the Causes of Human Operations, we shall discover them not to be free, but constrained: So that the Actions of Men not being voluntary, they are not therefore to be blamed for what they do, be it ever so bad."

Nonetheless, he still believed that some behaviors can be classified as good or evil: "Physical Good and Evil, then, do consist either in obeying, or in transgressing the most Sacred Laws of Nature: We obey them, in granting her whatever she desires; we transgress them, in opposing her just Pleasures, or in doing Violence to her." Civilized men, he thought, "have strayed away from the Laws of Nature in order to submit to other Laws of their own establishing, and opposite to the original ones in almost every Respect." He was especially contemptuous of the allegedly unnatural sexual mores of his society, calling virginity a "superlative evil."[26]

It is unclear how Radicati could square his determinism with the notion that humans had created "Laws of their own establishing," since those very laws must have been produced through naturalistic, deterministic processes. How can he appeal to his contemporaries to "obey" the laws of nature, if everyone's behavior is already determined by natural laws?

One moral standard he considered out of step with nature's mandates was the prohibition against suicide. He dismissed as nonsense the belief that humans are created in the image of God and therefore are special. He opined that "a Man more or a Man less" makes no difference in the cosmic scheme of things. Nature teaches us, he claimed, that if our life has become painful or troublesome, we can make use of the liberty and right of suicide that nature has bequeathed us. If one has no further prospects of future pleasure, it is entirely rational to commit suicide, he argued.[27]

French Enlightenment Thought on Suicide

Radicati was not alone in arguing for the permissibility of suicide. In eighteenth-century Enlightenment circles suicide was a frequent topic of conversation and debate.[28] Indeed, many of Radicati's ideas were cribbed (without attribution) from Montesquieu's *Persian Letters* (1721). At one point Radicati even quoted directly from Montesquieu's work (in quotation marks but without naming the source).

In *Persian Letters* Montesquieu, wanting to outsmart the French government's censors, placed his critique of many aspects of European culture and mores in the mouth of a Persian visiting France and writing to friends back home. In Letter LXXVII, Montesquieu's Persian protagonist Usbek (who probably represents Montesquieu's own position) objects to laws against suicide as unjust. He asks, "When I am opprest with Grief, with Misery and Contempt, why should I be hindered from putting an end to my sufferings?" He reasons further, "Life was given me as a favour; I may consequently give it back, when it is no longer so." It is not an affront against Providence, he wrote, "when I only alter the Modifications of Matter." He also argued that the misguided notion that our death has significance is born of pride, because "we do not see our own Insignificancy."[29] Montesquieu caught flak for defending the propriety of suicide, so in a later edition (1754) he tried to deflect criticism by adding a letter to Usbek from his Muslim correspondent, wherein the writer briefly (and not all that convincingly) defends laws against suicide.[30] On the whole, it seems pretty clear that Montesquieu's discussion of suicide, even in the later edition, was calculated to sway people in favor of legitimizing suicide. Radicati certainly thought so.

In his monumental *Philosophical Dictionary* (1764) Voltaire broached the topic of suicide in an article on "Cato on Suicide." Ambiguities abound in this article, which could simply reflect a nuanced position; or, more likely, they were the result of Voltaire attempting to evade censorship, an ever-present specter in eighteenth-century France. He portrayed Cato and other famous Romans who committed suicide as "heroes of true Rome, who preferred a voluntary death to a life which they believed to be ignominious."[31]

However, thereafter he criticized his contemporaries for committing suicide for foolish reasons, such as financial difficulties or bad health. Voltaire recommended activity as an antidote for suicide, and then stated, "The apostles of suicide tell us that it is quite allowable to quit one's house when one is tired of it. Agreed, but most men would prefer sleeping in a mean house to lying in the open air."[32] It seems that Voltaire is talking out of both sides of his mouth, claiming to agree with, but at the same time distancing himself from, these proponents of suicide. In some respects he seems to be discouraging suicide. However, from the closing of his article, it seems clear that he sympathized with a loosening of the moral prohibition against suicide. He there discussed the views of the Abbé St. Cyran (Jean Duvergier de Hauranne), who in the early seventeenth century wrote a work defending the permissibility of suicide in some circumstances. Voltaire quoted him as saying, "'A man may kill himself for the good of his prince, for that of his country, or for that of his relations.'" Voltaire seemed to agree with this position, as well as its corollary: if one can do this deed for the sake of others, one should also be allowed to do it for one's own benefit. Voltaire then stated, "I seek not to apologize for an act which the laws condemn, but neither the Old Testament, nor the New has ever forbidden man to depart this life when it has become insupportable to him." This last statement was probably intended to signal Voltaire's sympathy for the pro-suicide position, while averting censorship by officially stating he did not support it.[33]

A few years after Voltaire published these ideas about suicide, the French materialist thinker Baron d'Holbach included an unambiguous discussion of suicide in *The System of Nature* (1770). Of course Holbach rejected all religious arguments against suicide, but he also countered the argument that one should never abandon one's duty to society by killing oneself. Specifically, he argued that the social contract holds only if there is mutual advantage to be gained, and this contract is broken if the individual is filled with misery. Since Holbach, under the influence of Epicurean philosophy, considered happiness (defined as pleasure) the chief goal of life, he saw nothing wrong with committing suicide if one's life was no longer happy. "Death is to the wretched," Holbach wrote, "the only remedy for despair; the sword is then the only friend—the only comfort that is left to the unhappy."

Indeed, anyone who becomes despondent enough to commit suicide is simply obeying the dictates of nature, according to Holbach: "Nature, when it has rendered his existence completely miserable, has in fact ordered him to quit it." Not only did Holbach not consider suicide immoral; he (since he believed all human behavior was environmentally determined) believed it to be inevitable and irresistible.

To the objection that his ideas were dangerous because they might encourage suicide, Holbach disingenuously replied that people commit suicide because of their miserable circumstances, not because of philosophical ideas.[34]

Hume on Suicide

In 1746 the Scottish Enlightenment philosopher David Hume found an acquaintance, Major Alexander Forbes, bleeding after an attempted suicide. Hume called a physician, who bandaged the wounds, but Forbes died the following day anyway. In the interim Hume spoke with Forbes about his desire for suicide, and Hume told his brother in a letter, "Never a man exprest [sic] a more steady Contempt of Life nor more determined philosophical Principles, suitable to his Exit."[35] Apparently Hume understood that one's philosophy of life could influence one's decision to commit suicide.

About a decade later, Hume wrote the most thorough eighteenth-century defense of suicide. His essay, "On Suicide," completed around 1756, was controversial, and—because of concerns about possible legal action—Hume was unable to publish it during his lifetime. Some copies circulated clandestinely, and an English edition appeared for the first time in 1777, seven years after a French translation had been published.[36] In his essay Hume formulated some of the main arguments that are still used today by proponents of suicide and assisted suicide. He dismissed any religious objections, rejected the idea that human life has any special value, and asserted the primacy of individual autonomy. He also suggested that suicide could serve the purpose of social utility.[37]

As a religious skeptic, Hume began his essay by attacking religious prohibitions against suicide. First, he lashed out against "superstition," by which he meant the dominant Christian views of his time. "Superstition," he insisted, is an "inhuman tyrant" that deprives men of the pleasures of life. It makes men miserable, he complained, and then it will not even allow them to seek refuge from their sorrow through a self-inflicted death.

Hume then argued that God does not intervene directly in natural events, but rather superintends the universe through natural laws (it is not clear that Hume actually believed in any kind of God, including the deistic God he described here, so perhaps he is raising this point only for the sake of argument). Humans, he said, are themselves subject to the laws of nature, and yet they can and do intervene all the time in nature to alter the course of events. Hume reminded his readers that it is not criminal to alter nature by diverting the waters of the Nile or Danube. "Where then," he asked, "is the crime of turning a few ounces of blood from their natural channel?"

Hume seems to have overlooked that this could be used to justify murder just as easily as it could be used to excuse suicide. In any case, Hume was contemptuous of appeals to religious injunctions against suicide, stating, "'Tis impious, says the modern *European* superstition [i.e., Christianity], to put a period to our own life, and thereby rebel against our creator; and why not impious, say I, to build houses, cultivate the ground, or sail upon the ocean?"[38] Apparently Hume saw ending one's life as a rather prosaic deed.

Hume believed that suicide was morally permissible because he did not think human life had any special value. Most of his contemporaries believed that humans were created in the image of God and thus had a higher status than the rest of nature. Hume dispensed with this objection to suicide rather curtly: "But the life of a man is of no greater importance to the universe than that of an oyster."[39] Since he did not bother to provide any arguments to support this position, presumably Hume considered this self-evident (even though most people do not agree with his position, much less consider it self-evident). In any case, given his view that human life is insignificant, it is no wonder Hume did not object to suicide (but once again, with this philosophical basis, it is unclear how he could object to murder or genocide, either—after all, many humans kill myriads of oysters to eat without thinking anything about it).

Hume not only argued for the permissibility of suicide, but even considered suicide a duty in some circumstances. First, he thought it would be the right thing to do for people who find their lives burdensome. Hume wrote, "That suicide may often be consistent with interest and with our duty to ourselves, no one can question, who allows that age, sickness, or misfortune may render life a burden, and make it worse even than annihilation." Second, Hume suggested that if one's life has become a burden to others, it is best for society if that person commits suicide. He stated, "But suppose that it is no longer in my power to promote the interest of society; suppose that I am a burden to it; suppose that my life hinders some person from being much more useful to society. In such cases my resignation of life must not only be innocent but laudable." Hume claimed further that a person in such circumstances would be setting a good example for others by committing suicide.[40]

Opposition to Suicide during the Enlightenment

Hume and other voices approving of suicide were a tiny minority in the eighteenth century, but they did initiate a vigorous discussion about it in European society, especially among Enlightenment rationalists. Many religious leaders in eighteenth-century Europe, such as John Wesley, reasserted the traditional Christian prohibition against suicide and the accompanying Christian view that humans did have special status.

Some Enlightenment rationalists also rejected suicide as immoral. Immanuel Kant, the most famous academic philosopher of eighteenth-century Europe, was one of these. Kant provided both non-religious and religious arguments to support his position. Kant based his ethical philosophy on what he called the categorical imperative, which is: "Act only according to that maxim whereby you can at the same time will that it should become a universal law." Kant explained that because suicide cannot be a universal law, it must be immoral. Another moral principle that Kant embraced was the idea that humans should never be used as means, but should always be treated as ends in themselves. Suicide, Kant thought, treats oneself as a means, not an end, and thus is immoral.[41]

Kant also undercut one of the most prominent arguments in favor of suicide: the freedom or autonomy of the individual. He stated: "If freedom is the condition of life it cannot be employed to abolish life and so to destroy and abolish itself. To use life for its own destruction, to use life for producing lifelessness, is self-contradictory. These preliminary remarks are sufficient to show that man cannot rightly have any power of disposal in regard to himself and his life."[42] Kant recognized that suicide actually violates the freedom of the individual, because it ends the individual's life and thus the ability to exercise any freedom.

In keeping with the above, Kant rejected the contention that suicide is permissible to end a person's suffering. Kant spurned utilitarianism, the philosophy that judged the morality of an action based on its outcome—how much pleasure an action provides and how much pain it avoids (often summarized as "the greatest good for the greatest number of people"). Rather, Kant believed that one must do one's duty in life, no matter the pain or suffering involved. He wrote, "It is not necessary that whilst I live I should live happily; but it is necessary that so long as I live I should live honourably. Misery gives no right to any man to take his own life."[43]

Finally, Kant provided a religious argument against suicide. As an adult, Kant departed from the orthodox Christianity of his upbringing. He came, for instance, to exalt human reason above divine revelation. But he continued to believe in a God who created all things. A person who commits suicide, Kant thought, was rebelling against God by working in opposition to his divine purposes. Kant stated, "Human beings are sentinels on earth and may not leave their posts until relieved by another beneficent hand. God is our owner; we are His property; His providence works for our good."[44] In Kant's view, God knows what is good for us better than we do, so we should wait for him to take us out of this life, rather than taking matters into our own hands.

Conclusion

Though many Renaissance and Enlightenment thinkers still opposed suicide as immoral, these periods produced a shift in attitudes toward suicide. A small but growing number of intellectuals argued that suicide was morally unobjectionable, in part because they rejected the formerly dominant Christian morality. Utilitarian moral philosophy, which judged deeds by the pleasure-pain principle, became prominent during the Enlightenment. Utilitarian calculations often came out in favor of the permissibility of suicide in circumstances of distress and misery. Some Enlightenment thinkers, such as Hume, even claimed that suicide is morally good and beneficial in some situations.

None of these discussions dealt with euthanasia or assisted suicide per se; instead they focused on the right of the individual to commit suicide. However, the arguments in favor of suicide and the attitudes engendered by them would have significant implications for the issue of assisted suicide and euthanasia—voluntary and involuntary—as these issues arose in the nineteenth and twentieth centuries.

3. Euthanasia Meets Eugenics

When Anna Bollinger gave birth to a severely deformed infant in Chicago on November 12, 1915, the physician Harry Haiselden urged her and her husband to forgo life-saving surgery. The parents agreed, and five days later the baby died.

An investigation was opened and an autopsy performed. The six physicians on the coroner's jury found that "a prompt operation would have prolonged and perhaps saved the life of the child," that several of the child's defects could have been addressed by plastic surgery, and that there was "no evidence from the physical defects in the child that it would have become mentally or morally defective" (as Haiselden had claimed). However, though they found Haiselden's diagnosis faulty, they declined to criminally charge him, saying a surgeon should not be compelled to operate against his conscience.

Chicago Commissioner of Health John Dill Robertson, a surgeon who examined the baby eight hours before he died, likewise thought the child's physical problems had been exaggerated and probably could have been remedied; but even were that not so, Robertson argued, the standard civilizational premise "thou shalt not kill"—either by omission or commission—should not be abandoned.[1]

The mother, grief-stricken, died two years later. Haiselden, however, saw the death of the Bollinger baby as a triumph.

Killing the Disabled

Haiselden was a fervent supporter of the eugenics movement, which aimed at improving human heredity by restricting the reproduction of people with disabilities, whom eugenics proponents denigrated as "unfit" or "inferior" people or as "burdens." In his zeal to promote eugenics, Haiselden publicized the case of the Bollinger baby, getting considerable press coverage. Then, to spread his message even further, the following year he produced a movie, *The Black Stork*, featuring himself in the role of a physician who heroically refuses to operate on a disabled infant. In defending his position, the physician in the film remarks, "There are times when saving a life is a greater crime than taking one."[2]

The Bollinger baby case sparked a nationwide controversy. Many critics deplored Haiselden's callous attitude toward disabled people. The famous social reformer Jane Addams, for instance, insisted that people with disabilities had the same right to life as other people. She stated, "A physician or hospital board has not the right to assume the prerogative to say that any person shall be killed, but is required by the highest moral law to save every life that possibly can be saved."[3] Dr. John Dill Robertson said, "While it is true that mental and physical defectives have been a burden on society and will continue to be such, who is to say that the love and care bestowed on these defectives have not enriched the minds and hearts of those who have worked with and for these unfortunates, so that in the end the world is repaid for all the trouble they have caused us?"[4]

On the other hand, Haiselden had his defenders. The leading figure in the American eugenics movement, Charles Davenport, who had been professor of zoology at Harvard University before taking over the Cold Spring Harbor Lab, wrote that physicians should not "unduly restrict the operation of what is one of Nature's greatest racial blessings—death."

The flamboyant free-thinking lawyer Clarence Darrow (who later defended John Scopes at the famous Scopes Monkey Trial) argued, "Chloroform unfit children. Show them the same mercy that is shown beasts that are no longer fit to live."[5]

It may seem shocking, but the famous author Helen Keller publicly supported Haiselden, despite being blind and deaf, and despite her reputation as a disability rights advocate. She entered the public fray on Haiselden's behalf, stating that "a human life is sacred only when it may be of some use to itself and the world. The world is already flooded with unhappy, unhealthy, mentally unsound people who should never have been born."[6] Haiselden, Davenport, Darrow, and Keller represented a growing number of intellectuals and physicians in the early twentieth century who saw euthanasia as a way to improve humanity by ridding the world of hereditary "misfits."

Indeed Haiselden revealed in his autobiography that from his youth he had a rather dim view of people with disabilities. He admitted that he and some of his childhood friends had beaten up a mentally disabled woman. While expressing some regret about the incident, he did not seem repentant. He excused his behavior by claiming that a child "instinctively sees the menace in these wretched beings and adopts this means of fighting against it." He concluded that beatings, such as the one he dished out to this unfortunate woman, are "only part of the price that the inferior forms of human life must pay if they wish to live among their more fortunate brothers."[7]

Haiselden apparently never outgrew this attitude, for in 1915 he dismissed some people as having "lives of no value" and as "horrid semi-humans." He disparaged them further by stating, "Our streets are infested with an Army of the unfit—a dangerous, vicious army of death and dread." Haiselden saw himself as a hero rescuing society from this "vicious army." During the Bollinger baby controversy, Haiselden insisted that he advocated only passive euthanasia, i.e., allowing some people to die by withholding treatment. However, later he engaged in active euthanasia, since he gave lethal medication to a microcephalic infant.[8]

Fifty years before the Bollinger baby episode, the ideas and attitudes exemplified by Haiselden were almost non-existent in the United States and Europe. Throughout most of the nineteenth century, physicians in the US and Europe confronted dying by trying to ease pain and bring comfort to their patients. At the time this was called "euthanasia" (literally: "good death"). However, it was taboo for physicians to hasten the death of a patient. The prevailing medical ethics was encapsulated in the Hippocratic Oath that most physicians took, which stipulated that the physician could do no harm to patients nor put them to death.

One of the few exceptions we know of to the prevailing anti-euthanasia attitude was the German physician Carl Georg Theodor Kortum, who in 1800 published an article in a leading German medical journal advocating killing patients in their death throes. It is unclear if he actually practiced euthanasia. However, it is likely he did, since he claimed that a specific dose of laudanum would work, implying that he had experience using it to kill one or more patients.[9]

The modern euthanasia movement, which redefined the word "euthanasia" to mean "mercy killing," arose in 1870, when public discussion began in both Britain and Germany about the propriety of physicians killing patients. While some euthanasia advocates championed physician-assisted suicide or voluntary euthanasia, others began promoting the idea that some people with disabilities should be killed without their consent (involuntary euthanasia). Indeed, by the early twentieth century, euthanasia proponents were more often pressing for the coercive killing of disabled people (that is, without permission from the disabled persons), rather than assisted suicide, though often they endorsed both kinds of killing.

Why did some Americans and Europeans begin advocating assisted suicide and/or involuntary euthanasia for people with disabilities in the late nineteenth and early twentieth centuries? Historians agree that it had nothing to do with any new medical technologies, nor with changes in how people died. Indeed, the debate over euthanasia began outside the medical profession. Rather, the euthanasia movement arose because of changing attitudes about life and death, which were brought about by intellectual shifts in Europe and the United States. Most importantly, Western thought was becoming more secularized by the mid- to late-nineteenth century, so the influence of Christian prohibitions on suicide declined, and Christian compassion toward people with disabilities waned. Many secular intellectuals no longer believed that humans were created in the image of God, so they did not regard human life as sacred. They also no longer regarded Christian ethics as binding and often tried to formulate new ethical standards.

In the best historical analysis of the euthanasia movement in America to date, Ian Dowbiggin explains, "Trends such as eugenics, positivism, social Darwinism, and scientific naturalism had the effect of convincing a small yet articulate group in the early twentieth century that traditional ethics no longer applied to decisions about death and dying."[10] These secularizing tendencies altered people's understanding of the meaning of life and death and helped give rise to the euthanasia movement.

Darwinian Death

One secularizing influence—Darwinism—played a particularly powerful role in helping erode the Judeo-Christian sanctity-of-life ethic. Dowbiggin highlights this point by stating, "The most pivotal turning point in the early history of the euthanasia movement was the coming of Darwinism to America."[11] Nick Kemp, who has written the best book on the history of the British euthanasia movement, concurs with Dowbiggin. He writes, "While we should be wary of depicting Darwin as the man responsible for ushering in a secular age we should be similarly cautious of underestimating the importance of evolutionary thought in relation to the questioning of the sanctity of human life."[12] Indeed, Dowbiggin and Kemp both portray the pioneers of the euthanasia movement as mostly atheists, agnostics, or something similar, whose ideas were heavily influenced by Darwin's theory of biological evolution.

In Germany the euthanasia movement arose out of similar secularizing tendencies. One of the leading experts on the euthanasia debates in Germany before World War I, Hans-Walter Schmuhl, explains, "By giving up the conception of the divine image of humans under the influence of the Darwinian theory, human life became a piece of property, which—in contrast to the idea of a natural right to life— could be weighed against other pieces of property."[13] Not only did most

Darwinists see humans as just another animal, but many believed that morality had evolved, undermining any objective moral standards, such as Judeo-Christian ethics. Most Darwinists in the late nineteenth century also embraced human inequality, believing that some races and individuals were more evolved than others and, therefore, more valuable than others. Many races and individuals they deemed "unfit," and they considered death a positive force that would cull these "inferior" people from the human race, leaving the "fit" to propagate the species. Most early euthanasia proponents saw killing people with disabilities as just a natural, normal part of the Darwinian struggle for existence.[14]

Another powerful influence on the early euthanasia movement was eugenics ideology, which emerged first in the 1860s under the leadership of Francis Galton, a cousin of Charles Darwin. While reading Darwin's book, *The Origin of Species*, it occurred to Galton that from generation to generation humans could vary biologically— moving in what he considered either a positive or a negative direction. He then proposed that we should consciously aim at improving the human species by fostering the reproduction of those with "good" traits, while restricting the reproduction of those who are allegedly inferior biological specimens. Galton did not suggest killing anyone to improve the species, and not all eugenics proponents agreed with euthanasia as a proper eugenics measure. However, the eugenics movement's tendency to value only some human lives—rather than all human lives—together with its negative attitudes toward people with disabilities, helped spawn attitudes congenial to euthanasia. After all, based on their Darwinian vision of nature, most eugenicists saw death as a beneficent force that rids the world of those who are inferior. The eugenics movement gained many adherents in the early twentieth century, especially among psychiatrists and physicians, many of whom regarded mental illnesses as hereditary and incurable. Some of the more radical members of the eugenics movement played leading roles in the euthanasia movement as well.

In the Anglo-American world, Samuel Williams, an obscure British schoolteacher, fired the opening salvo in the public debate over euthanasia when he published a controversial article in the *Essays of the Birmingham Speculative Club* in 1870. Though this journal was usually not very widely read, his essay must have touched a nerve, for it generated many responses—both positive and negative—in more influential venues. Williams's essay also appeared as a pamphlet titled *Euthanasia*, and it sold so well that it went through four editions by 1873. Williams proposed in his essay that physicians be allowed to administer a lethal dose of medicine to patients with incurable, painful illnesses, but only if the patients desired it. Williams dismissed the traditional Christian idea that all human life has value, but instead maintained that "it may well be doubted if life have any sacredness about it, apart from the use to be made of it by its possessor."[15] He stressed the importance of understanding the Darwinian struggle for existence among humans, and he argued that those "who perished due to illness, disability, or old age were merely succumbing to the fate of all 'weak' creatures who lost out to the 'hardiest' individuals."[16] Invoking the Darwinian struggle for existence as a justification for getting rid of the sick and weak would be a common refrain by euthanasia proponents in the following decades.[17]

One of the most prominent responses to Williams's essay came from Lionel Tollemache, who published "The Cure for Incurables" in 1873 in *Fortnightly Review*, an influential publication. Tollemache agreed with Williams. He thought the time had come for people to toss the "sanctity of life" idea on the ash-heap of history. He shared the advice of the ancient Roman Epicurean poet Lucretius, who encouraged the elderly to welcome death, because nature could recycle their material to fashion younger bodies. He also invoked more modern ideas:

> And, in a somewhat similar spirit, modern science informs us that in an overcrowded population there is a sharp struggle for existence: so that an unhealthy, unhappy, and useless man is in a manner hustling out of being, or at least out of the means of enjoyment, someone who would probably be happier, healthier, and more useful than himself.[18]

Thus Tollemache invoked Darwinian biology to defend euthanasia. He also seemed to be shaming anyone who would be selfish enough to continue living when they are no longer "useful." This theme of a person's "usefulness" continues to surface in today's discussions of euthanasia and assisted suicide.

Williams and Tollemache, however, faced many critics. Their ideas were considered extremely radical in the 1870s, and most of the articles published in the ensuing debate rejected their position. Certainly most of the religious leaders in Europe and the United States rejected their brand of euthanasia. The medical community was not very receptive, either, as most still faithfully adhered to the Hippocratic Oath. In 1873 the famous British anthropologist Edward Tylor joined the debate by attacking Williams's position, arguing that killing the elderly was a characteristic of primitive societies. He believed that civilized societies had advanced beyond this practice, and he portrayed euthanasia as a relapse into barbarism.[19]

A couple of decades later, in 1894, the British philosopher F. H. Bradley published an essay in the *International Journal of Ethics* promoting involuntary euthanasia as a new form of punishment for those deemed biologically inferior. Bradley also referred to this "punishment" as "social surgery" or "moral surgery." Bradley claimed that he derived this new vision of punishment directly from Darwinian processes, since evolution produces improvement through selecting individuals with favorable traits and eliminating those with unfavorable characteristics. Bradley explained, "The right and the duty of the organism to suppress its undesirable growths is the idea of punishment directly suggested by Darwinism." He overtly rejected the notion of individual rights, subordinating them to the interests of the community. He stated, "Assuming here that the welfare of the community is the highest end and law, and assuming that selection among varieties is necessary to that welfare, I intend briefly to apply these ideas to the subject of punishment." He remonstrated against the Christian doctrine of the sacredness of human life and insisted that humans are not equally valuable. Thus, in his view, "social amputation," as he also called it, should be directed against people with disabilities. "Surely, then, the least cruel, the most merciful course of conduct—the best means in our power to diminish suffering—is to regard nothing but the conditions of general advantage" of the community, he argued. "And as to these conditions Darwinism offers a positive doctrine. It teaches, in a word, the necessity of constant selection.... That way consists in the destruction of worse varieties, or at least in the hindrance of such varieties from reproduction."

In closing the essay, Bradley rejected the suggestion that these "worse varieties" of humans should be confined (as in asylums), since "it seems wrong to load the community with the useless burden of these lives." He expressed contempt for those with mental illnesses, remarking, "I am disgusted at the inviolable sanctity of the noxious lunatic." Rather, he proposed that we kill them: "But still our remedy would have to utter and to enforce this sentence, 'You and you are dangerous specimens; you must depart in peace.'"[20] Bradley's focus was thus on involuntary euthanasia for those that society deems inferior biologically.

The same year that Williams published his controversial essay in Britain in support of assisted suicide, the Darwinian biologist Ernst Haeckel became one of the first German intellectuals to seriously propose infanticide for babies with serious disabilities. In the second edition of his book on evolutionary theory, *Natürliche Schöpfungsgeschichte* (*Natural History of Creation*), Haeckel did not overtly advocate infanticide, but he did promote it in a back-handed way: "If someone would dare to make the suggestion, according to the example of the Spartans and Redskins, to kill immediately after birth the miserable and infirm children, to whom can be prophesied with assurance a sickly life, instead of preserving them to their own harm and the detriment of the whole community," he remarked, "our whole so-called 'humane civilization' would erupt in a cry of indignation."[21]

Haeckel, both in this book and many subsequent works, stressed that humans are not equal, and this inegalitarian attitude would become widespread in the eugenics and euthanasia movements.

In his 1904 book, *Lebenswunder* (*The Wonders of Life*), Haeckel admitted that his 1870 comments about Spartan infanticide were indeed intended to encourage the practice in modern society. To justify this position he appealed to his theory of evolutionary recapitulation, which claimed that as organisms develop embryologically, they go through the stages of their evolutionary history. Thus, when humans were conceived as single cells, they were equivalent to protozoa, and as they developed further, they would traverse a fish stage, a reptile stage, and so forth. Even a newborn infant, Haeckel thought, was at a lower evolutionary stage than an adult human. Thus a baby's life is no more valuable than some kind of animal in the infant's evolutionary ancestry. Haeckel used similar reasoning to devalue the lives of people with mental disabilities. He argued that people with hereditary mental illnesses had not developed beyond an animalistic stage, so killing them was not morally problematic. He condemned the idea that we should always preserve human life, "even if it is completely worthless." He lamented that his society was wasting its resources by keeping thousands of mentally ill people alive. Better, he insisted, to give them a shot of morphine and end their lives. He suggested that the decision for these acts of involuntary euthanasia should rest with a commission of physicians.[22]

In that book Haeckel also advocated assisted suicide for those with incurable illnesses. He rejected the idea that suicide is "self-murder," which is the literal translation of the German word; he preferred the term "self-redemption." He pointed out that we kill animals in misery, so he thought we should do the same for humans who want our assistance in ending their lives. He stated, "Likewise we have the right, or if one will, the duty, to prepare an end for the dire sorrow of our fellow human being, if severe illness without hope of improvement makes their existence unbearable and if they ask us for 'redemption from evil.'"[23]

Haeckel thus promoted voluntary euthanasia for those with incurable, painful illnesses, and involuntary euthanasia for those with hereditary mental illnesses.

We, the Superior

Another German intellectual contributing to the emerging euthanasia movement was the death-of-God philosopher Friedrich Nietzsche. Nietzsche's existentialist philosophy with its stress on free will was fundamentally incompatible with Haeckel's deterministic worldview. However, they agreed on some fundamental issues that related to euthanasia.

Nietzsche, like Haeckel, was radically opposed to human equality, and he believed that the individuals he deemed superior—whom Nietzsche called Overmen or Supermen—should rule over those who are inferior and even destroy many of them. In his 1887 book, *The Genealogy of Morals*, Nietzsche wrote, "To sacrifice humanity as mass to the welfare of a single stronger human species would indeed constitute progress."[24] About the same time he also stated, "The great majority of men have no right to existence, but are a misfortune to higher men."[25] Nietzsche's philosophy is often classified as one of the German "Philosophies of Life" (*Lebensphilosophie*), but in Nietzsche's case, this meant life only to the intellectual aristocracy, the Overmen. These exalted individuals could create their own morality of strength, power, and domination to replace the allegedly archaic Christian ideas of love and compassion. His philosophy exulted in oppression, enslavement, and even death for the masses, as long as it benefited the Overmen.

In harmony with his inhumane views, Nietzsche praised suicide and infanticide as noble acts. A section of his 1885 book *Thus Spake Zarathustra* was titled, "On the Free Death." He enjoined his readers to kill themselves at a time of their choosing, rather than waiting for death. This was a way for them to exert their will to power. He encouraged them to commit suicide when they are in a state of victory, rather than waiting until they are feeble. He lamented that many people stay alive too long.[26]

In 1888 Nietzsche wrote a brief section in *Twilight of the Idols* on "Morality for Physicians," where he promoted assisted suicide. He also encouraged doctors to stop keeping people alive if their lives are past redemption. The new medical ethic he proposed "demands the most inconsiderate pushing down and aside of degenerating life—for example, for the right of procreation, for the right to be born, for the right to live."[27] Though he did not overtly tell physicians they should kill infirm patients, his remarks seem to imply it. In an 1882 work Nietzsche had already indicated his support for killing people with disabilities. Therein he included a parable about a man who approaches a saint with a "miserable and deformed" child in his arms. The saint advises him to kill the child, which disappoints the man. Other by-standers reprove the saint for saying this, but he replies, "But isn't it crueler to allow it to live?"[28] The way this is presented it seems clear that Nietzsche is using the saint to present his own views. Though sometimes cloaking his teaching in parables, Nietzsche was promoting euthanasia.

The Right to Die

The first German to write an entire essay on assisted suicide and euthanasia, published in 1895 as a 53-page pamphlet, was Adolf Jost, a student at the University of Göttingen who was about twenty years old. Jost's father was a physician who committed suicide and left behind a letter encouraging his son to follow his example when life reached a point where it was no longer pleasant. In his pamphlet, *The Right to Die*, Jost argued that not all human lives have value. He mentioned that some people struggle "with the torment of deadly disease, mental illness, or social distress, and often their death would be the best thing for them and their society." Jost believed the value of a human life should be measured by the utilitarian pleasure-pain principle. If life is more pleasurable than painful, it has positive value. He explained that this functions at two levels: the pleasure and pain in individual experiences, and the pleasure and pain the individual causes society. If the pain outweighs the pleasure for both the individual and society, then that person's life has negative value. Such people should have the "right to die."

Jost considered mentally ill people a burden on both themselves and society, so even though they could not consent, he still thought society should kill them. He admitted, however, that resistance against this practice was considerable, so he suggested beginning with the legalization of voluntary assisted suicide.[29] Though Jost was promoting what he called the "right to die," he seemed to suggest that some people have a "duty to die," and if they did not fulfill their duty, society should do it for them without their consent. In light of his disdain for those with mental problems, it is ironic that Jost himself became mentally ill at age thirty-three and died (of natural causes) soon afterward.[30]

Another discussion about euthanasia and assisted suicide flared up in Germany in 1913 in the journal of the Monist League, an organization founded by Haeckel and like-minded thinkers who rejected body/soul dualism, insisting that humans did not have any kind of soul separate from the body. One of their members, Roland Gerkan, was suffering from a terminal disease, and this prompted him to write an article calling for the legalization of euthanasia. He died soon after writing his essay. Gerkan's plea was only for voluntary euthanasia. He recommended that the individual wanting euthanasia should first apply to the judicial authorities and then be examined by three physicians, who would verify that that person was suffering from a terminal illness. If the physicians determined that it was most likely a terminal illness, a physician could help the patient commit suicide.[31] The prominent chemist, Wilhelm Ostwald, who edited the Monist League's journal, agreed wholeheartedly with Gerkan, though another member of the League wrote a rebuttal.[32]

Before World War I broke out in 1914, euthanasia was still considered a radical proposal in Europe. Between 1901 and 1915 the *British Medical Journal* published seven editorials or articles on euthanasia, and all were uniformly negative toward it.[33] The medical profession elsewhere rejected it, too. The broader public was also still decidedly opposed. But the discussion about euthanasia and assisted suicide had begun, and they gained more support as time went on.

America Joins the Debate

Just as in Europe, euthanasia—in its current definition of ending a person's life for the good of the person or society—was almost universally condemned in the United States in the early and mid-nineteenth century. Only in the late nineteenth century did a few radical voices emerge advocating euthanasia and assisted suicide. In 1879 the South Carolina Medical Association became the first body of physicians in the United States to discuss euthanasia, when they directed a committee to study the issue. Reflecting the dominant views at the time among both physicians and the broader public, the committee rejected euthanasia. However, one member of the South Carolina Medical Association disagreed, remarking, "Euthanasia was as sure to be accepted as was the doctrine of evolution and that would be as surely as the Copernican system in astronomy."[34] This comment reflected the self-perception of euthanasia proponents as scientific and progressive, in opposition to their benighted, retrograde opponents.

In 1891 Felix Adler became one of the first American intellectuals to propose that assisted suicide be permitted for those suffering with terminal illnesses. Though his father was a rabbi, he embraced a non-theistic worldview while earning his doctorate at the University of Heidelberg. However, Adler ardently believed that morality could be grounded on a secular worldview, so he established the Ethical Culture Society in 1877 to promote a secular ethic. In 1891 he lectured on "The Ethics of Suicide" to the School of Ethics in Plymouth, Massachusetts. He morally opposed most suicides, but he allowed for some exceptions. Specifically, he recommended that physicians be allowed to provide a poisonous potion to patients with terminal illnesses. He suggested that a panel of judges and physicians make determinations about each case, making sure the case is terminal. Adler's proposal horrified Charles Deems, the president of the American Institute of Christian Philosophy, and undoubtedly many other contemporaries. Deems called Adler's position a "foolish and wicked doctrine."[35]

Three years later the famous agnostic lawyer and orator Robert Ingersoll published an open letter challenging the Christian prohibition on suicide. He insisted that it is only natural that people in misery would want to kill themselves. He rejected the allegedly antiquated notion that since God has created us humans, we should remain alive until God brings death upon us. On the contrary, he stated, "In many circumstances a man has the right to kill himself. When life is of no value to him, when he can be of no real assistance to others, why should a man continue? When he is of no benefit, when he is a burden to those he loves, why should he remain?" He even took this argument a step further by intimating that sometimes it would be morally wrong not to commit suicide. Ingersoll maintained that happiness is the only good, and since he did not believe in an afterlife, he thought that "death is not so terrible as joyless life." (Although he argued for the moral propriety of suicide, he did not broach the issue of assisted suicide in this piece.) Ingersoll's letter aroused a bevy of critics, who published their objections to his controversial broadside.[36]

In January 1906 controversy over euthanasia erupted again when the prominent physician Walter Kempster confessed in the press that he had given a patient close to death a fatal dose of morphine "in order to prevent further suffering." Kempster was public health commissioner for Milwaukee, and he had testified at the trial of President Garfield's assassin. Within a couple of months bills had been introduced into the Ohio and Iowa legislatures to legalize physician-assisted suicide, though both failed to pass. In the ensuing controversy, the proponents of assisted suicide did not appeal to individual rights or autonomy, but rather to what was best for the collective welfare.

Indeed, the discussion conflated voluntary euthanasia for people who had painful terminal illnesses—the original issue for Kempster—with coercive euthanasia for people with hereditary illnesses. For instance, in a *New York Times* article in February 1906, Lurana Sheldon, a writer who had earlier been a physician, harshly criticized those who wrote letters to the *Times* "denouncing the proposed extermination of a certain class of incurables." As a physician Sheldon had experience with the mentally ill, and referred to such people in her article as "poor creatures from whom all trace of the human has fled, and who cumber the earth merely as animated lumps of flesh." Killing such people is not only an act of "true humanity to the helpless sufferer," in her view, but also would bring "relief from hideous, moral-blunting service" to those caring for them.[37]

By the early twentieth century some prominent Progressive intellectuals and leaders, such as Jack London and Eugene Debs, embraced euthanasia and assisted suicide.[38] However, the vast majority of the medical community was decidedly against the idea. From 1901 to 1915 the *Journal of the American Medical Association* carried six editorials and comments, plus one article, on euthanasia. All of them rejected it.[39] This is not to say, however, that all physicians opposed euthanasia at this time. In his book *Heredity and Human Progress* (1900), the physician William Duncan McKim argued that science militated against the "unreasonable dogma that *all* human life is intrinsically sacred." Dowbiggin explains that "McKim's secular and scientific rationales for euthanasia in the early twentieth century signaled a revolutionary challenge to literally hundreds of years of Judeo-Christian teaching about the dignity of human life."[40]

Conclusion

Under the influence of secularization the euthanasia movement began its first tiny steps in 1870. Most supporters of euthanasia in the late nineteenth and early twentieth centuries were atheists or agnostics who considered their worldviews scientific and progressive. Darwinism played a prominent role in their thought, and they relied on Darwinian concepts to underpin their euthanasia ideology. Since they no longer believed that God had created humans in his own image, they discarded the Judeo-Christian emphasis on the sanctity of human life. Thus they saw nothing wrong with suicide if the individual wished it. Indeed, some of them even suggested that people with chronic, terminal illnesses should commit suicide, in order not to burden those who had to care for them.

Euthanasia proponents also rejected the notion of human equality and inalienable human rights, such as the right to life. Eugenics ideology, which was founded upon Darwinian precepts, bred negative attitudes toward those who were deemed inferior biologically, such as the mentally ill. Thus, many early advocates of euthanasia argued that killing people with serious hereditary illnesses was not only permissible, but desirable. The focus of the early euthanasia movement was more on the collective good than on individual rights and autonomy. Thus, many of the early proponents called for involuntary euthanasia, as well as assisted suicide.

4. Euthanasia Gains Ground in the US and Britain

FACING THE FINAL STAGES OF TERMINAL BREAST CANCER, THE noted feminist author Charlotte Perkins Gilman opted to kill herself with chloroform, rather than wait for death to arrive. She notified her family and friends about her decision ahead of time, and none of them tried to dissuade her. On the contrary, they expressed support and understanding for her desire to end her life. On August 17, 1935, she carried out her plans, quickly dying from inhaling a large dose of chloroform.[1] She left behind a suicide note that not only explained and justified her deed, but also expressed the hope that society would become more accepting of suicide for those with terminal illnesses. She wrote:

> Human life consists in mutual service. No grief, pain, misfortune, or "broken heart" is excuse for cutting off one's life while any power of service remains. But when all usefulness is over, when one is assured of unavoidable and imminent death, it is the simplest of human rights to choose a quick and easy death in place of a slow and horrible one. Public opinion is changing on this subject. The time is approaching when we shall consider it abhorrent to our civilization to allow a human being to die in prolonged agony which we should mercifully end in any other creature. Believing this open choice to be of social service in promoting wiser views on this question, I have preferred chloroform to cancer.[2]

Indeed, Gilman was right that attitudes in the US and Europe seemed to be changing by the mid-1930s, and—though still facing considerable popular opposition—euthanasia was gaining acceptance, especially among the intellectual elites.

Getting Organized

As we have already seen, a small number of activists were already promoting euthanasia in the late nineteenth century. It took some time, however, before the idea gathered momentum. Only in the 1930s did euthanasia and assisted suicide gain sufficient adherents in the US and Britain for organizations to form devoted to legalizing the practice. These organizations focused mostly on legalizing assisted suicide and voluntary euthanasia for people with terminal illnesses who desired it, in part because they did not think the public was ready to sanction involuntary euthanasia. However, many euthanasia proponents were stalwart believers in eugenics who also supported involuntary euthanasia for people with disabilities, especially those having mental illnesses.

Who were these organizers and members of the growing euthanasia movement? Most were progressives or radicals who spurned the Judeo-Christian religious tradition and its morality, including its stress on the sanctity of human life. Some of them identified as humanists, atheists, or agnostics, and many did not believe in any kind of afterlife, so they considered death final. Among the more religious euthanasia proponents, Unitarians predominated, though there were also some Protestant clergy with liberal theological inclinations who endorsed euthanasia. Politically, euthanasia advocates tended to be left-of-center, sometimes on the radical fringe.

Gilman, in fact, is fairly representative of early twentieth-century euthanasia advocates. In 1923 she published a book, *His Religion and Hers: A Study of the Faith of Our Fathers and the Work of Our Mothers*, which attacked Christianity and other major world religions as tools of male domination. She was especially indignant that most religions tend to focus a good deal of attention on an afterlife; instead, she thought, religion should concern itself with improving life in this world. She wanted to replace what she considered male-dominated, outmoded religions with a new religion based on natural laws, especially biological evolution, which she called "the greatest of all [ideas], changing as it did our whole concept of life."

Indeed she based her new religion's morality on promoting evolutionary progress. "The new motherhood," she explained, "will submit to nothing but its own great governing law—to maintain and improve the human race." A critical component of her plan was biological improvement, so eugenics played a key role. She insisted that women should select their mates consciously with the goal of improving the human species, making as their slogan: "No more morons!" Indeed, Gilman explained that in her religion, eugenics was paramount: "But mere selection of the fittest is barely a beginning of what may be done in race-improvement. Most of all we need the constant teaching that this improvement is a religious duty, *the* religious duty above all."[3]

In *His Religion and Hers* Gilman did not discuss the implications of her new religious principles for suicide or euthanasia. However, in other writings—and in her own death—she divulged her support for voluntary and involuntary euthanasia. As she explained in her autobiography, her views were shaped in part by her experience with her father's deteriorating condition before his death. Her father suffered from dementia late in life, before passing away in 1900. She lamented his mental decline, and suggested, "It is not right that a brilliant intellect should be allowed to sink to idiocy, and die slowly, hideously. Some day when we are more civilized we shall not maintain such a horror."[4] Already in 1912 she published an article advocating voluntary euthanasia for a woman who was requesting death because she was paralyzed and had been experiencing excruciating pain for three years.[5] A few months earlier she had written a brief article, "Good and Bad Taste in Suicide," where she deplored the "bad taste" of those who throw themselves under a train, but praised the "good taste" of those who use chloroform to commit suicide peacefully.[6] As noted above, this was how she would later kill herself, so she was not just being amusing.

Gilman's most important contribution to the euthanasia debate was an article, "The Right to Die," published in a major journal soon after her suicide. An abbreviated version appeared in 1937 in *Readers Digest*, so her views gained considerable attention.[7] In that article she admitted that not all kinds of suicide are morally acceptable. However, she explained, "If men or women are beyond usefulness, feel that they are of no service or comfort to any one but a heavy burden and expense, and, above all, if they suffer hopelessly, they have a right to leave."

After arguing that people have a right to end their own lives, she then defended capital punishment, which, according to her, should not be called punishment at all. Rather, it is the "elimination of diseased parts from our body politic," an "operation on the social body." Immediately after defending society's right to kill criminals, she stated, "The same position may be taken in regard to the incurable idiot or maniac.... Why should we not painlessly remove them?" She apparently did not believe that the lives of mentally ill people had any value. Perhaps she was thinking of her father when she wrote, "When intelligent consciousness is gone forever, the man is gone, and the body should be decently removed." She concluded her plea for involuntary euthanasia for those she deemed "unfit" with utilitarian considerations: "But the dragging weight of the grossly unfit and dangerous could be lightened, with great advantage to the normal and progressive. The millions spent in restraining and maintaining social detritus should be available for the safeguarding and improving of better lives." By calling certain people "unfit," "dangerous," and "social detritus" Gilman—reflecting views rather common in the eugenics and euthanasia movements—expressed contempt for those with mental disabilities. As with many other eugenics enthusiasts, she had a collectivist mentality, placing the interests of society above the rights of individuals.[8]

The Euthanasia Society of America

On April 18, 1937, humanist Charles Francis Potter issued a press release calling for the formation of an organization that would press for "the legalization of mercy-killing." His plea was carried by the *Washington Post*, as well as other newspapers. Nine months later he announced that he had successfully founded the National Society for the Legalization of Euthanasia, which was soon renamed the Euthanasia Society of America (ESA). Its purpose, according to Potter, was to put pressure on state legislatures and the US Congress to legalize mercy-killing for those with incurable illnesses. The new organization often debated whether to also promote involuntary euthanasia for the mentally ill, because many ESA members favored this policy. However, they ultimately decided to focus exclusively on legalizing voluntary euthanasia, figuring it would be easier to sell to the public.[9]

According to historian Ian Dowbiggin, Potter was the most important and effective leader in the American euthanasia movement in the first half of the twentieth century.[10] In the 1920s he was a progressive Unitarian minister in New York City who rejected the traditional Christian teachings about miracles and an afterlife. He was firmly committed to evolutionary theory and even testified on behalf of the defense at the famous Scopes Monkey Trial in 1925. According to his autobiographical account, in 1924 he did not approve of euthanasia. However, he changed his mind gradually for two reasons: 1) he gained experience with people suffering in the throes of death; and 2) his study of religion caused him to reject religion altogether, and this led him to alter some of his views on morality.[11] The changes in Potter's religious doctrines caused him to abandon his ministry in the Unitarian Church in 1929 and establish the First Humanist Society of New York. In 1933 he was one of the original thirty-four signers of the Humanist Manifesto, and he remained committed to humanism for the rest of his life.

From his base in New York City, Potter recruited many luminaries and activists to participate in the ESA. Many of his associates and friends from the humanist society joined, and secular progressives tended to predominate. However, he also tried to build a broad coalition that included liberal Protestant pastors and Jewish rabbis. Mrs. Ann L. Mitchell of Garden City, New York, agreed to finance the organization, and this allowed Potter to open an office on Broadway.

The original board of the ESA was a rather colorful cast.[12] Eleanor Dwight Robertson Jones was a leading birth control activist who had wrested control of the American Birth Control League from Margaret Sanger in the late 1920s. A leader in the humanist society, Harry Elmer Barnes, was a controversial historian whose hobby horse was denying that Germany bore any responsibility for the outbreak of World War I. (Later he made a similar claim regarding World War II, and denied the Holocaust.) The sociologist Frank H. Hankins signed the Humanist Manifesto and served as president of the American Sociological Society in 1938. The geneticist Clarence Cook Little, who served as president at the University of Maine and the University of Michigan in the 1920s, was so committed to eugenics and hereditarian explanations[13] that he served as president of the American Eugenics Society for a time. In the later phases of his career he acted as a mouthpiece for the tobacco industry, claiming that cancer was hereditary and that smoking had no ill effects on health.

ESA board member and biologist Oscar Riddle was featured on the cover of the January 9, 1939, issue of *Time* magazine, with a brief caption accompanying his photo on the cover: "Evolutionist Riddle. 'All men are created unequal.'" Like many other eugenics proponents, Riddle rejected human equality, and this anti-egalitarianism infused the euthanasia movement. Another original board member, the economic statistician Walter F. Willcox, was also keen on refuting human equality in his work on racial statistics.[14] Finally, the Jewish Rabbi Sidney E. Goldstein embraced the ESA cause and joined the board.[15]

Because of his writing career and his leadership of the humanist society, Potter was extremely busy, so he soon resigned the presidency of the ESA. However, he continued to promote euthanasia in lectures and in media interviews. One of his successors as president of the ESA, the New York City neurologist Foster Kennedy, considered involuntary euthanasia the real pressing issue of the day. In a 1942 article on sterilization and euthanasia, Kennedy warned against some aspects of Nazi Germany's sterilization program, because he believed it was too far-reaching. According to Kennedy, sterilizing some highly functioning "feeble-minded" people would rob society of a useful labor force, and sterilizing all manic-depressives might impoverish humanity by stymying creativity.

Nonetheless, Kennedy insisted that "we have too many feeble-minded people among us," so we need to find measures to reduce their number. He approved of sterilization for some mentally disabled people who might be able to perform some simple labor, but then he posed the question, "What to do with the hopelessly unfit?" His answer: "I am in favor of euthanasia for those hopeless ones who should never have been born—Nature's mistakes." Kennedy proposed that at age five, upon the parents' request, a board of physicians would review multiple times the case of someone who is "defective," and then kill him or her if they deemed it appropriate.

Interestingly, while clearly advocating involuntary euthanasia for those with severe mental disabilities, Kennedy admitted that he had come to oppose voluntary euthanasia for those with terminal illnesses. He explained that earlier in his career he had been sympathetic with voluntary euthanasia, but his experience as a physician convinced him that many misdiagnoses occur, so patients might still live productive lives, even after being diagnosed as terminal.[16] Kennedy's stance on voluntary versus involuntary euthanasia put him at odds with others in the ESA, so he only served as president for two months in 1939.[17]

Kennedy was not the only ESA member to promote involuntary euthanasia, however. Indeed, many ESA members saw euthanasia as a means to cull humanity of its "inferior" specimens. This would necessarily involve involuntary euthanasia for those with congenital illnesses. When World War II broke out, Ann Mitchell, who served as secretary and primary funder of the ESA, wrote to a colleague that she hoped the war would last a long time, so it would precipitate "euthanasia as a war measure, including euthanasia for the insane, feebleminded monstrosities." She called the Nazi murder of mentally ill children in Poland a "great blessing."[18] However, most ESA members—even if they privately agreed with involuntary euthanasia—recognized that the American public was not ready to go that far. Thus they maintained their strategic focus on voluntary euthanasia as a first step.

Another famous and influential member of the ESA was Margaret Sanger, founder of Planned Parenthood. Her primary passion was promoting birth control, which she thought would solve many of the ills of society. However, she claimed that euthanasia was similar in one respect to birth control. While birth control helped to "bring entrance into life under control of reason," euthanasia hoped "to bring the exit of life under that control."[19]

Despite Potter's efforts and optimism, the ESA failed in its early legislative attempts. Potter claimed that in its early phases the ESA recruited almost two thousand physicians in New York state, as well as over fifty eminent clergymen from a variety of denominations.[20] However, public opposition to euthanasia remained strong in the US. Most physicians rejected euthanasia, and in response to ESA lobbying for the legalization of euthanasia in New York state, in 1950 the New York State Medical Society passed a resolution denouncing euthanasia. Instead they affirmed, "Life is God-given and precious."[21] The Roman Catholic Church and most Protestant churches also continued to reject euthanasia and assisted suicide.

A Famous Biologist Promotes Euthanasia

Though most scientists and physicians in early twentieth-century America opposed euthanasia, one of the most prominent scientists in the United States during that time, Alexis Carrel, promoted euthanasia as beneficial. Carrel was a Nobel Prize-winning biologist twice featured on the cover of *Time* magazine in the 1930s. A November 18, 1935, article in *Time* on "The Right to Kill" reported, "The Rockefeller Institute's famed Nobel Prizeman Alexis Carrel declared that sentimental prejudice should not obstruct the quiet and painless disposition of incurables, criminals, hopeless lunatics."[22]

In a 1935 lecture (published in 1936), Carrel discussed "The Mystery of Death." In that speech he explained that death is a necessity, because it prevents overcrowding and "liberates the new generations from the burden of the old." By keeping people alive longer, he claimed, we have "almost suppressed natural selection," by which "the strong and the intelligent persisted, and the great races developed." Carrel suggested that by keeping people alive, medicine was counteracting this beneficent process and creating a problem: "The weaklings have become artificially the equal of the strong. And civilized countries are encumbered with those who should be dead." Though he did not overtly propose killing these "weaklings," he clearly expressed negativity toward their staying alive.[23] Carrel's biographer sums up his position in this lecture by claiming that he "argued that medically prolonging a person's life is worse than death and is a burden to civilized countries."[24]

In his 1935 book *Man, the Unknown*, Carrel explicitly promoted euthanasia, but only for criminals, including those who have committed crimes because of their insanity. He lamented that modern developments, such as medicine, had preserved the lives of "many inferior individuals," such as criminals and people who are insane. He also asserted that people in the lower classes in the US are biologically inferior, since, he claimed, "most members of the proletarian class [in the US] owe their situation to the hereditary weakness of their organs and their mind." This threat of the proliferation of the so-called inferior people led him to suggest that "the propagation of the insane and the feeble-minded... must be prevented." However, Carrel did not set forth specific policy proposals to make this happen, aside from his euthanasia proposal: "Those who have murdered, robbed while armed with automatic pistol or machine gun, kidnapped children, despoiled the poor of their savings, misled the public in important matters, should be humanely and economically disposed of in small euthanasic institutions supplied with proper gases. A similar treatment could be advantageously applied to the insane, guilty of criminal acts." Like many other eugenics advocates, Carrel was more interested in promoting involuntary euthanasia for those he deemed "inferior" than voluntary assisted suicide.[25]

The British Voluntary Euthanasia Legalisation Society

Just as in the United States, eugenics considerations powerfully shaped the British discussion of euthanasia in the early twentieth century. In their zeal to improve the human species biologically, early euthanasia advocates in Britain often promoted involuntary euthanasia for those they deemed biologically inferior or "unfit." For example, in the early twentieth century the psychiatrist and asylum director Richard J. A. Berry advocated killing people with mental illnesses. Such arguments were not, it seems, without effect. Nick Kemp, in his historical study of the British euthanasia movement, confirms this, stating, "The increasingly pronounced negative bent of eugenics [i.e., the desire to stop the reproduction of those deemed 'inferior'] between the wars facilitated discussion of mercy-killing for the more severe cases of mental defect." Kemp even makes the case that in the 1920s support for involuntary euthanasia preceded and gave impetus to the movement to legalize voluntary euthanasia.[26]

Nonetheless, the first organized effort to legalize euthanasia in Britain arose in the 1930s and focused on voluntary euthanasia. Charles Killick Millard, the Medical Officer of Health in Leicester, England, initiated the movement in 1931, when he delivered a presidential address to the Society of Medical Officers of Health advocating the legalization of voluntary euthanasia. The following year he promoted the same agenda in a lecture to the British Medical Association.

This well-respected physician was known for his "progressive" attitudes, since he was already an avid supporter of birth control and eugenics. He soon recruited several others in Leicester, including the physician C. J. Bonds and the Unitarian minister R. F. Rattray, to form the Voluntary Euthanasia Legalisation Society (VELS) in 1935. Bonds, a vice-president of the British Eugenics Society and a member of the National Birth Control Council, became the first chairman of the VELS.[27] The organization promoted only voluntary euthanasia, in part because they thought this would be less controversial than involuntary euthanasia and thus easier to sell to the British public. However, many of its members also supported involuntary measures. Rattray, for instance, in 1934 stated that there was "a strong case for euthanasia without the knowledge of the patient in the case of children suffering hopeless and terrible torment, births of an abnormal kind. Surely it is not justified to prolong these lives, letting them be a prey on normal people, undermining their health and sanity."[28]

The VELS quickly attracted progressive luminaries to support its mission, including novelist H. G. Wells, author and pacifist Vera Brittain, playwright George Bernard Shaw, Marxist professor Harold Laski, biologist (and later the founding director of UNESCO) Julian Huxley, and historian G. M. Trevelyan.[29] Another prominent supporter of the VELS, novelist Virginia Woolf, had earlier expressed utter disregard for the sanctity of human life, confiding to her diary in 1915:

> On the towpath we met & had to pass a long line of imbeciles. The first was a very tall young man, just queer enough to look twice at, but no more; the second shuffled, & looked aside; & then one realized that every one in that long line was a miserable ineffective shuffling idiotic creature, with no forehead, or no chin, & an imbecile grin, or a wild suspicious stare. It was perfectly horrible. They should certainly be killed.[30]

Instead of showing compassion for these people with disabilities, Woolf—who knew nothing about their lives—apparently saw herself as so superior to them that she wanted them dead, merely because they offended her sensibilities. In an unfortunate twist of dramatic irony, Woolf suffered from mental problems that ultimately led her to stuff her pockets full of rocks and walk into a river to end her life.

Woolf was not the only VELS supporter who devalued the lives of people with disabilities. The prominent progressive physician Havelock Ellis, an ardent eugenicist, was forthright about his antipathy toward people with disabilities. In a 1948 collection of his essays, *On Life and Sex*, he overtly endorsed "killing the unfit," in a passage opposing militarism, where he stated:

> But the militarists may be cheered to think that even when war is totally abolished, there is still a place in morality for killing, and an infinitely more humane place than that occupied by murder in war, that is to say by killing the unfit, not by killing the fit. Only so can we be true to the instincts that have created Man. It is the aim of eugenics to eliminate, so far as possible, the unfit stocks, which by their constitutional defects lower the level of human achievement and increase the difficulties of social life.[31]

He then lamented that one of the "unfortunate results of Christianity" had been the rejection of infanticide. The ban on infanticide, according to Ellis, was currently producing "injury to our race" and causing the "misery of the victims of our supposed 'humanitarianism.'" He urged his contemporaries to jettison the "quaint superstition" of keeping alive "the most hopelessly maimed and defective of new-born infants." He hoped for a return to the Greco-Roman practice of killing disabled infants.[32]

Ellis also promoted voluntary euthanasia, and when he was dying in 1939, he decided to hasten his death. According to one of his biographers, "Not because he was afraid of bearing pain, but because he believed that man should hold the Key of Death, he decided to make his own end. It should be a blow struck for euthanasia."[33] Ellis asked his mistress to help him commit suicide, but—even though she agreed with him that it was morally permissible—she hesitated, because she was concerned about the legal ramifications. Because of her delay, he died a natural death.[34]

In 1936 the VELS introduced its Voluntary Euthanasia Legalisation Bill into the British House of Lords for debate. The bill would have authorized designated medical personnel—upon the patient's request—to kill patients over twenty-one years old who faced severe suffering from a fatal illness. The peer who moved the bill, Lord Ponsonby, lamented that Lord Moynihan, a physician and an esteemed member of the House of Lords, had recently passed away, so he could not move the bill. Ponsonby then explained the rationale for the bill by quoting Moynihan, who had served as a president of the VELS: "Briefly our desire is to obtain legal recognition for the principle that in cases of advanced and inevitably fatal disease, attended by agony which reaches, or oversteps, the boundaries of human endurance, the sufferer, after legal inquiry and after due observance of all safeguards, shall have the right to demand and be entitled to receive release."[35]

The two physicians in the House of Lords at that time opposed the bill, as did most of the medical community in Britain. William Cosmo Gordon Lang, the Archbishop of Canterbury, also spoke against the bill, because he considered suicide immoral. He admitted that there could be exceptions to this general rule, but he opposed enshrining the acceptance of suicide into law.[36]

One of the arguments that Lord Ponsonby had advanced in favor of the bill was that it would enable patients to unselfishly remove the burden on others that their suffering imposed. The Earl of Crawford expressed astonishment at this line of reasoning, insisting that this measure would likely inflict more pain than it would relieve. He asserted, "I contemplate with profound distress the unconscious pressure which will be placed upon the sick man to persuade him that he is in the way and that he should evacuate this life."[37] The bill was defeated, thirty-five to fourteen.

After the 1936 defeat of the VELS bill, Millard redoubled his efforts to legalize euthanasia. He announced in 1940 that the VELS had compiled a list of about 850 supporters "who have achieved distinction in their respective spheres of life." Support from religious leaders was also slowly growing. He hoped to reintroduce the bill after the war was over.[38] However, by 1950, when the bill was reintroduced into the House of Lords, the intellectual and social climate was not as favorable toward euthanasia as it had been during the 1930s. In 1950 both the World Medical Association and the British Medical Association issued statements condemning euthanasia, and all five physician members of the House of Lords opposed its legalization. Most Britons were shocked by Nazi atrocities that came to light in the wake of World War II, including the Nazi euthanasia program, which had resulted in the murder of about 200,000 Germans with disabilities, as well as tens of thousands more in German-occupied countries. Since some prominent British supporters of voluntary euthanasia also endorsed killing people with disabilities, this cast a pall over the whole initiative.[39] The 1950 attempt to legalize euthanasia in the UK failed miserably, and subsequent attempts were also unsuccessful.

Personhood: Not for Everyone

Support for euthanasia and assisted suicide also waned in the United States in the aftermath of World War II, as religious devotion grew and as Americans reacted against the Nazis' murderous euthanasia campaign that had targeted people with disabilities. The World Medical Association issued a strong condemnation of euthanasia in 1950, and American medical societies wholeheartedly agreed. The Roman Catholic Church remained a staunch opponent of euthanasia and assisted suicide, and in 1949 the American Council of Churches, consisting of fifteen Protestant denominations at that time, denounced euthanasia.[40] A 1950 poll of Americans revealed that support for euthanasia had declined since the 1930s.[41]

However, during the 1950s a new champion for euthanasia and assisted suicide emerged. Joseph Fletcher is widely regarded as an influential founder of the field of bioethics in the mid-twentieth century.[42] His views on euthanasia gradually gained greater acceptance—especially among intellectual elites—over the course of the late twentieth and early twenty-first centuries. He also contributed to the upsurge of ethical relativism in the 1960s through his controversial book, *Situation Ethics*, published in 1966.[43]

While he was in high school, Fletcher embraced socialism, and he considered himself a Marxist during his student years at the University of West Virginia. However, in his autobiography he claimed that throughout his life he had an aversion to creeds and a deeper commitment to the philosophy of pragmatism as propagated by William James and John Dewey. (Pragmatism taught that morality was determined by the practical effects of actions, not by objective, unchanging principles.) His pragmatism eroded his commitment to Marxism. It also undermined his relationship with Christianity, which was always rather superficial.[44]

In the early decades of Fletcher's career, he was an Episcopal priest and professor of theology and ethics at the Episcopal Theological School in Cambridge, Massachusetts. According to his own account, he chose this vocation not because of religious devotion, but because as an avowed socialist he thought it would provide him a platform to promote social reform. In the 1960s, however, he re-examined his relationship with Christianity and concluded that "the whole thing was weird and untenable." The Christian doctrines of creation, the Fall, and redemption were absurd, he thought. In 1967 he told his colleagues at the Episcopal seminary that he was an unbeliever, and thereafter he overtly embraced humanism, signing the Humanist Manifesto II (which endorses the right to suicide) in 1973.

Thus, though in Fletcher's early writings he cloaked some of his arguments in religious terminology, by his own later admission the true underpinnings of his thought were secular. He confessed in his autobiography that his situation ethics was "utterly independent of Christian presuppositions or beliefs." He then explained, "My own ethics, as I tackled value problems and the right-wrong issues posed by medicine and biological innovations, was essentially humanist—humanist in the sense of nontheist. Like Protagoras I saw man as the measure of things, the determiner of value and truth, not God or a revelation of any kind."[45]

In 1954 Fletcher wrote his first major work on bioethics, *Morals and Medicine*. In chapter seven, "Euthanasia: Our Right to Die," he defined euthanasia as "merciful release from incurable suffering." He defended voluntary euthanasia, not only as a fundamental right, but also as an act of compassion. The primary argument that Fletcher devised to promote euthanasia has come to be known as personhood theory, because Fletcher insisted that not all human beings are full-fledged persons. He claimed that qualifying as a person involved more than just being a living human being with functioning organs. He asserted that human beings are not persons from the moment of conception or even the moment of birth; rather, they gradually develop into persons. Thus, some humans are persons, and others are not.

What would qualify one as a person, then? According to Fletcher, the key attribute of a person is self-consciousness, though he also mentioned other defining traits of personhood, such as moral freedom, self-awareness, and being self-determined. Based on these considerations, Fletcher claimed that those with "fatal and demoralizing illnesses" should have the "right to die" with a physician's assistance.[46]

It seems likely that Fletcher's 1954 claim that he was only supporting voluntary euthanasia for those in the throes of a terminal illness was based on tactical considerations, not conviction, because taken to its logical conclusion his personhood theory clearly justifies involuntary euthanasia. Indeed, in later works Fletcher admitted this, promoting abortion, infanticide, and involuntary euthanasia on the basis of his personhood theory. In his 1979 book, *Humanhood*, for instance, he stated, "Humans without some minimum of intelligence or mental capacity are not persons, no matter how many of their organs are active, no matter how spontaneous their living processes are.... A human vegetable is not a person, not truly a human being."

Fletcher delineated fifteen traits that he thought a human had to possess in order to be a full-fledged person with all the rights pertaining thereunto: 1) minimal intelligence; 2) self-awareness; 3) self-control; 4) sense of time; 5) sense of futurity; 6) sense of the past; 7) capability to relate to others; 8) concern for others; 9) communication; 10) control of existence; 11) curiosity; 12) change and changeability; 13) balance of rationality and feeling; 14) idiosyncrasy; and 15) neocortical function. Fletcher never explained, however, how many of these traits a person had to have, or how much of each of these traits a person needed, in order to be a real person. Nonetheless, Fletcher was convinced that neither a fetus nor a newborn infant had enough of these traits to be considered a person, so he justified abortion and even infanticide, stating, "It is reasonable, indeed, to describe infanticide as postnatal abortion."[47]

Fletcher also articulated the utilitarian position "that human happiness and well-being is the highest good or *summum bonum*, and that therefore any ends or purposes which that standard or ideal validates are just, right, good." The highest moral value, he thought, was "human well-being, either by maximizing happiness or minimizing suffering." Because of this, he insisted that "it is better to be dead than to suffer too much or to endure too many deficits of human function."

Two points are worth underlining. First, Fletcher forthrightly argued that in cases where killing promotes human well-being and reduces suffering, we not only are allowed to do it, but *should* do it. Second, Fletcher argued that even if certain human beings are persons, if their death would result in greater good or less evil, then they "might properly be sacrificed on the principle of proportionate good."[48]

Because of his philosophical support for euthanasia, Fletcher became an early member of the Euthanasia Society of America, which changed its name to the Society for the Right to Die in 1974. He even served as president of that organization for a couple of years in the mid-1970s.[49] The Society for the Right to Die did not make any headway in its legislative battles before the 1990s. However, Fletcher had a powerful impact in academe on the budding field of bioethics, winning many disciples for his personhood theory.

Legal Scholar Pushes Euthanasia in the UK

Just as in the United States, the euthanasia movement in Britain faced stiff headwinds in the 1950s. As noted earlier, the VELS succeeded in introducing another voluntary euthanasia bill into the House of Lords in 1950, but it met an ignominious defeat.[50] At that time there were five physicians in the House of Lords, and all opposed the bill.[51] Another setback for the VELS (which was renamed the Euthanasia Society in 1955) was the 1952 death of Millard, its forceful founder and leader.[52]

Not long after, in 1955, the eminent British legal scholar Glanville Williams gave a lecture to the Euthanasia Society, which he served as vice president for a time.[53] He also defended euthanasia to a larger academic audience through his book *The Sanctity of Life and the Criminal Law*, originally published in 1957. Williams's book was based on lectures he gave in 1956 while a visiting professor at Columbia University in New York City. Earlier, from 1945 to 1955, Williams had been a law professor at the University of London, and in 1966 he received a professorship at Cambridge University.

In *The Sanctity of Life and the Criminal Law*, Williams spurned the idea that human life is sacred, regarding this view as an archaic religious vestige that modern society should discard. He claimed that anyone arguing against euthanasia on the basis of the commandment, "Thou shalt not kill" was illegitimately imposing a "theocratic morality" on society. Unfortunately, however, Williams showed little understanding of the Christian ethical positions that he rejected. For instance, he erroneously claimed that the primary reason the Roman

Catholic and other Christian churches have opposed infanticide historically is their doctrine that baptism confers salvation, and thus infanticide would send a soul to hell. (This is mistaken on two levels. The Catholic Church does not teach that unbaptized infants go to hell.[54] And since Catholics also oppose infanticide after baptism, Glanville's claim is obviously incorrect.) In place of the Christian sanctity-of-life ethic, Williams favored an ethical philosophy of pragmatism and/or utilitarianism.[55]

Williams admitted that it is immoral to kill another human being. However, he made exceptions for abortion, infanticide, and voluntary euthanasia, for two reasons. First, he founded his general prohibition against murder on pragmatic and utilitarian considerations, such as social necessity and public security, and he did not believe these three forms of killing violated such concerns. For instance, he endorsed the position of Jeremy Bentham, who is often considered the father of utilitarian ethical theory, that because infants feel no fear of murder, it is not immoral to kill them.[56]

Second, Williams argued that "what is a human being is not so simple a question as it may sound." He claimed that science had blurred the boundaries between human and non-human: "To the eye of science, nature is a continuum, and man, like everything else, is part of a process." He specifically appealed to an evolutionary view of humanity, including Haeckel's theory of recapitulation, when describing some newborn infants as "monsters," who "may belong to the fish stage of development, with vestigial gills, webbed arms and feet, and sightless eyes." Some disabled infants, in Williams's view, are "worthless or even repellent," so he saw nothing wrong with killing them.[57]

Williams proposed that physicians be allowed to administer voluntary euthanasia to patients. The poor quality of a person's life, especially if the person is suffering intense pain, he argued, could legitimately override the legal prohibition against killing:

> It is good that men should feel a horror of taking human life, but
> in a rational judgment the quality of the life must be considered.
> The absolute interdiction of suicide and euthanasia involves the
> impossible assertion that every life, no matter what its quality or

circumstances, is worth living and obligatory to be lived. This as-sertion of the value of mere existence, in the absence of all the activities that give meaning to life, and in face of the disintegration of personality that so often follows from prolonged agony, will not stand scrutiny. On any rationally acceptable philosophy there is not ethical value in living any sort of life: the only life that is worth living is the good life.[58]

Williams's ideas gained greater currency in the late twentieth and early twenty-first centuries, as British society became increasingly secularized. However, efforts to legalize voluntary euthanasia have continued to fail in Britain, where, as of this writing, euthanasia and assisted suicide continue to be illegal.

Conclusion

The movement to legalize voluntary euthanasia gained ground in the 1930s, both in the US and in Britain. Euthanasia proponents formed organizations, not only to spread the pro-euthanasia message, but also to lobby governments for legalization. While these organizations restricted their efforts to legalize voluntary euthanasia, many of the leading figures in the euthanasia movement also endorsed involuntary euthanasia. They believed involuntary euthanasia would help improve the human species by halting the reproduction of those they deemed biologically inferior. By the 1950s these organizations were facing stiff headwinds, as most physicians and politicians, together with the majority of the British and American public, continued to oppose the legalization of any kind of euthanasia.

5. Nazis Target "Life Unworthy of Life"

Late in the summer of 1941, nurses at an institution in Hadamar, Germany, a small city northwest of Frankfurt, led a group of people with disabilities into the basement, where they were directed into a gas chamber. After the door was closed, a physician turned the valve to release carbon monoxide gas into the room, asphyxiating everyone inside. This murderous procedure had been repeated many times since Nazi officials had converted the Hadamar asylum into a center for mass killing in January 1941. Indeed, it had occurred so often that by this time, the medical personnel in Hadamar had killed their ten-thousandth victim. Instead of covering their faces in shame, the perpetrators decided to celebrate their accomplishments. Everyone working there gathered in the basement around the ten-thousandth corpse, listened to a brief oration by a fellow employee mockingly dressed like a priest, and then received a free beer.[1] The corpse was later incinerated, like all the others before it.

Altogether, the Nazi campaign to murder people with disabilities resulted in the death of about 200,000 Germans plus about 80,000 people in Poland, the Soviet Union, and France, and likely many more in other German-occupied territories.[2] The final victim was murdered at a mental asylum in Kaufbeuren, a small city in southern Bavaria, on May 29, 1945, about a month after the Americans had occupied that area. The American authorities were horrified to learn that people with disabilities were still being killed, even after the collapse of the Nazi regime, and they put a stop to it.

At his subsequent trial, Valentin Faltlhauser, the psychiatrist directing the Kaufbeuren facility, claimed—as did many other medical personnel in the dock for murder and crimes against humanity—that he was motivated by compassion and was thus morally justified in killing two thousand people with mental illnesses at his institution.[3]

How is it that the Nazi regime was able to find so many physicians, nurses, and other personnel not only willing, but even enthusiastic, about carrying out these grisly tasks?

Helping Evolution Along

As we have already seen, in the late nineteenth century the social Darwinist idea that nature eliminates weak and sick organisms in order to produce something better had already begun to gain traction among European thinkers. More radical voices soon began advocating involuntary euthanasia—killing those deemed "unfit"—as a way to help out the evolutionary process. In Germany the debate over euthanasia reached a new level in 1920 with the publication of the controversial book *Permitting the Destruction of Life Unworthy of Life*, coauthored by the psychiatry professor Alfred Hoche and the legal scholar Karl Binding. In this book, Binding and Hoche called people with mental disabilities "life unworthy of life," with Binding going so far as to claim they are "not only absolutely worthless, but existences with negative value." Not only did he argue that their lives were useless and a burden to others, but he insisted that caring for them is misguided, because it squanders the resources of the "better" people.[4]

In his section of the book, Hoche reiterated many of Binding's points and called for a new kind of medical ethics that placed less value on the lives of individuals.[5] In an autobiographical work Hoche explained why he thought individuals were not all that important. He stated that in nature, "the continued existence of the species is everything, the individual is nothing; she [nature] carries on an immense waste of seeds, but the individual, after she has given it—the mature one—opportunity to pass on its seed to the future, she heedlessly lets die; it is for her purposes without value."[6] With such arguments Hoche hoped to undermine his society's concern for the value of every individual, including those with disabilities.

Note that as a trained psychiatrist, Hoche should have been committed to helping people with mental illnesses, but instead he reviled them as "completely valueless" and "mentally dead" people who have forfeited all legal rights, including the right to life.[7]

A Shift in Medical Ethics

Binding and Hoche's book faced considerable opposition and critique when it appeared. Nonetheless, it did begin to make the idea of euthanasia—both voluntary and involuntary—respectable in academic discourse. While the vast majority of German physicians remained staunchly opposed to euthanasia in 1920, a growing number of medical professors and physicians thereafter began to find the idea more palatable.

Even among those physicians who resisted euthanasia, many embraced eugenics with its stress on biological inequality and the primacy of the collective good over individual rights. This led to a transformation of medical ethics, whereby the physician became the guardian of the health of the nation, not just the healer of individuals.

It was this collectivist version of medical ethics that the Nazis emphasized in a medical ethics course they began requiring for all medical students in 1939, the same year Hitler authorized the killing of people with disabilities. In collectivist thought, promoting the biological vitality of the nation and race was the primary moral consideration that trumped all other concerns. The welfare of the individual surrendered to the national good. This inverted medical ethics, which in previous eras had focused on the well-being of the individual patient.[8]

By the time Hitler required physicians who were willing to kill, a considerable cadre of medical professionals who approved of euthanasia were available for recruitment.

Hitler's Darwinian Enthusiasm

We do not know if Hitler ever read Binding and Hoche's book, but his attitude in the 1920s clearly mirrored their views (and the views of many other scholars).[9]

Hitler was committed to a social Darwinist vision of human interaction, whereby the "fittest" outcompete the "unfit" in the universal struggle for existence, which inevitably results in the death of multitudes. He was fanatically committed to eugenics ideology, which taught that eliminating the weak and sick would benefit the human species, elevating it to higher evolutionary levels.[10]

For example, in 1923, while discussing measures to halt the reproduction of people with disabilities, Hitler stated, "The preservation of a nation is more important than the preservation of its unfortunates."[11] In a speech five years later he rejected the idea that individuals have a right to life. Rather, he claimed, struggle is the law of nature, and the only rights one has are those gained through competition with others. He asserted that in this Darwinian struggle for existence, "The weaker must die, the earth is only for the healthy, and only they have the right to life."[12]

In 1928–29 Hitler strongly implied that he supported killing people with disabilities. In his *Second Book*, which remained unpublished until after his death, he admired the ancient Spartans for their practice of infanticide. He commented:

> The abandonment of sick, frail, deformed children—in other words, their destruction—demonstrated greater human dignity and was in reality a thousand times more humane than the pathetic insanity of our time, which attempts to preserve the lives of the sickest subjects—at any price—while taking the lives of a hundred thousand healthy children through a decrease in the birth rate or through abortifacient agents, subsequently breeding a race of degenerates burdened with illness.[13]

Even more ominously, in a major speech at the Nuremberg Party Congress in August 1929, Hitler declared:

> If annually Germany would produce a million children and dispose of 700,000 to 800,000 of the weakest, then in the end the result

would possibly even be an increase in strength. The dangerous thing is, that we ourselves interrupt the process of natural selection and thereby slowly deprive ourselves of the possibility to increase our population.

He then praised Sparta as the "clearest racial state in history."[14]

This is a shocking prescription—killing 70 to 80 percent of children—and Hitler undoubtedly did not mean it to be a guide to policy. However, it shows how radically committed he was to eliminating the weaker members of society in order to increase the biological strength of the nation overall.

Sterilization First

Clearly, then, before coming to power in 1933, Hitler already had a genocidal mentality toward those with congenital disabilities. However, he knew that killing people with disabilities would be frowned upon by many Germans. Thus, he initially settled on a less radical policy: compulsory sterilization for people with congenital illnesses.

Compulsory sterilization had already been implemented in many parts of the United States, as well as in Denmark. Leading eugenics proponents in the US, Germany, and elsewhere were thrilled in July 1933 when the Nazi regime promulgated the Law for the Prevention of Hereditarily Diseased Offspring, which required that people with certain congenital disabilities be sterilized.[15] This law not only targeted individuals with congenital mental and physical illnesses, but it also included in its scope those with chronic alcoholism and anyone identified as "feeble-minded," an elastic category if there ever was one.

Leading German scientists and physicians helped craft this law, and many doctors participated in its implementation, either by rendering decisions about whom to sterilize, or by performing the operations. Over the brief course of the Third Reich an estimated 350,000 to 400,000 individuals were compulsorily sterilized. This was about one out of every two hundred Germans.

Eugenics ideology and the sterilization program helped pave the way for the later mass murder of disabled people. It reinforced the view that some humans, especially those with disabilities, are inferior. The Nazis encouraged this view, taking steps designed to arouse an abhorrence of "unfit" people. They sent schoolchildren on field trips to mental asylums. They made documentary films about hereditary illnesses. *Opfer der Vergangenheit* (*Victim of the Past*), a 1937 film produced jointly by Goebbels's Propaganda Ministry and the Racial Policy Office, included this commentary:

> In nature everything weak unfailingly perishes. In the last few decades we have sinned terribly against this law of natural selection. We have not only preserved the life [of the weak], but we have even allowed them to reproduce. All this misery could have been prevented, if we had previously prevented the reproduction of the hereditarily ill.

Further, the film insisted that people with mental illnesses "are lower than any animal."[16]

Nazi eugenics propaganda also continually stressed that people with disabilities are a financial burden.

At times eugenics propaganda even implied that death—not just sterilization—was an appropriate solution. German biology teachers, for example, were provided a poster designed to explain to their classes the necessity of the sterilization program. It carried the title: "Elimination of the Sick and Weak in Nature." Two pictures on the poster illustrated this point: one showed a raptor with its dead prey and the other depicted a man cutting down a sickly-looking tree. In both cases the "elimination" was occurring through death, not sterilization.

If the pictures were not enough to underscore the point that death is nature's way, the caption below the pictures made it explicit: "Whatever cannot withstand the demands of existence, is destroyed." As in this instance, Nazi propaganda continually stressed that we should emulate nature—even when it means death to the sick and weak—because this will result in biological improvement in the long run.[17]

The Killing Begins

Although Hitler discussed killing people with disabilities with some of his associates in the mid-1930s, he hesitated to turn his ideas into policy—until he was prompted by a request from a father:

> In February 1939 a severely disabled son was born to Richard Gerhard Kretschmar. Kretschmar asked a local physician to kill his baby boy. The doctor refused on the grounds that this was illegal, so the father wrote directly to Hitler requesting permission to have his baby euthanized. The Führer responded by directing his personal physician, Karl Brandt, to travel to Leipzig, see whether he concurred with the diagnosis, and if so, allow the physicians there to kill the baby.[18]

Brandt, in the course of his university studies and medical training, had imbibed the social Darwinist and eugenics mentality that pervaded the fields of biology and medicine in early twentieth-century Germany. In fact, he completed his studies in 1926–28 at the University of Freiburg, where he studied under the euthanasia advocate Alfred Hoche.

Brandt adopted Hoche's views on euthanasia, so when Hitler asked him to intervene in the Kretschmar case, he was already convinced that it was morally justifiable—maybe even morally praiseworthy—to kill people with disabilities. According to Brandt's biographer, Ulf Schmidt, for Brandt and his associates, "Death became a core value in their overall belief system. The death of the weakling, the frail and incurable sick was believed to be of intrinsic value in relation to the greater good."

Brandt saw himself as an idealist striving to benefit humanity.[19] When he was put on trial in 1947 for helping lead the Nazi euthanasia program, he defended himself, stating, "I am deeply conscious that when I said 'Yes' to Euthanasia I did so with the deepest conviction, just as it is my conviction today, that it was right. Death can mean relief. Death is life—just as much as birth. It was never meant to be murder."[20]

Whatever his intentions, Brandt orchestrated the program that killed multitudes of innocent men, women, and children. On July 25, 1939, Gerhard Herbert Kretschmar became the first victim of the Nazi euthanasia program, after Brandt authorized the killing.

This episode seems to have whetted Hitler's appetite for more killing, for he authorized Brandt and Philipp Bouhler, a high-ranking Nazi Party functionary, to organize a secret children's euthanasia program to kill disabled infants. Just a few weeks after Kretschmar's death, the Nazi regime decreed that physicians must register all infants born with disabilities. Many physicians likely supposed this was for the purpose of collecting scientific data. However, the forms submitted were actually intended to decide the fate of the infant. Medical experts recruited by Brandt, Bouhler, or other Nazi officials examined these forms, often in a rather hasty and perfunctory manner, to determine whether the infant should live or die.

In order to carry out the killing operations in this child euthanasia program, which began sometime around October 1939, the physician Hans Heinze set up a special ward in his institution at Brandenburg-Görden (west of Berlin), where the authorities brought the children they had condemned to death. Eventually more than twenty other institutions and hospitals throughout Germany had similar wards that followed Heinze's approach. The infants were normally killed by being poisoned with overdoses of medication, though some were starved to death. By 1945 medical personnel had killed about five thousand children in this children's euthanasia program.

Extending Euthanasia to Adults

The children's euthanasia program was just the first phase of killing. Hitler quickly expanded the killing operations to include disabled adults. In order to assure participating physicians that they would not be prosecuted for murder, Hitler even signed a secret decree in October 1939 authorizing the euthanasia program.

He backdated the memo to September 1, the date Germany launched its invasion of Poland, probably to imply that the euthanasia program was linked to the war effort. Indeed, in Hitler's mind euthanasia and expansionism were connected, because the goal of his military expansion was to clear away people of "inferior" races and make space for the settlement of the allegedly superior Aryan race, while the aim of euthanasia was to rid Germany of "inferior" individuals. Hitler's brief memo stated, "Reichsleiter Bouhler and Dr. Brandt are commissioned to extend the authority of those physicians they designate so that mercy killing may be administered to those who according to human judgment are incurably sick, after diagnosis of the condition of their illness."[21]

Before Bouhler and Brandt were able to initiate their euthanasia program, however, the mass killing of people with disabilities began under different auspices. Hitler had sent SS and police squads (known as Einsatzgruppen) into Poland behind the regular army. Their task was to round up and shoot Polish political leaders, intellectuals, priests, and others the Nazis considered dangerous elements of the Polish population. Beginning immediately after the invasion of Poland, these units executed about fifty thousand Poles (seven thousand of them Jewish) by December 1939.[22] In late October 1939 these killing squads expanded their scope to include people with disabilities, and they began clearing asylums in occupied Polish territories. The first episode occurred near Neustadt, a city near Gdansk (known to the Germans as Danzig) that had been part of Germany before World War I but had been given to the recreated country of Poland in 1919. SS units near Neustadt rounded up patients from various institutions in the vicinity and shot them in mass graves dug by Polish prisoners. Within a month this SS unit had murdered about 3,500 asylum patients.[23]

In late 1939 another SS unit under Herbert Lange began clearing asylums, first in Wartheland, a Polish territory that Germany annexed during the war, and later elsewhere in the east. Lange's unit pioneered the use of the gas van for mass killing. At first they used carbon monoxide canisters, but later they simply piped the exhaust fumes from the truck into the sealed cargo space. They could pack forty victims into the gas vans at a time and transport them to mass graves.[24] Lange would later use his mass killing techniques to annihilate thousands of Jews, when he was appointed the first commandant of the first Nazi death camp in Chelmno, which began murdering Jews in December 1941.

Aktion T4: Secrecy and Death

Meanwhile, in 1939 Brandt and Bouhler recruited the economist Viktor Brack as director of the euthanasia program with the psychiatrist Werner Heyde leading the medical side of the operation (in December 1941 Heyde was replaced by another psychiatrist, Paul Nitsche).

The adult euthanasia program required a good deal more coordination than the child euthanasia program, because of the greater numbers involved, so they set up a secret organization to administer it. It was code-named T4 because its offices were located in Berlin at Tiergartenstrasse 4. To hide their activities T4 created front organizations to handle logistics, such as collecting data and transporting patients. They sent forms to all institutions caring for people with disabilities, asking for detailed information about each patient. Over forty physicians, including nine university medical professors, then evaluated the forms to determine if the patient should live or die. The physicians making these decisions never met the patients, and often they processed the forms rapidly. One psychiatrist processed over two thousand forms in less than twenty days, while managing his normal duties of directing a mental asylum.[25]

Brandt later claimed that at the outset he and Hitler had discussed killing methods, and when Hitler asked him what the most humane method was, Brandt replied that carbon monoxide was probably the best. In any case, either in December 1939 or January 1940, Brandt, Bouhler, and Brack, together with several leading T4 physicians, conducted an experimental gassing at a facility in Brandenburg. They apparently considered the gassing a success, because in addition to the Brandenburg institution, they immediately constructed a gas chamber at another facility in Grafeneck, south of Stuttgart. By June 1940 they had added two other institutions to carry out the T4 mass murder operation, one at Hartheim in Austria and another at Sonnenstein, near Dresden.

Most of the victims of the Nazi euthanasia program shared three main characteristics: they were institutionalized, had an illness that was hereditary (or one that was presumed to be hereditary), and could do little or no useful work. Many were mentally ill or epileptic, but some had congenital physical illnesses, such as blindness or deafness.[26] One boy was killed because he was born without arms. Some were institutionalized—and then euthanized—because of their drug addiction.[27]

Once an individual was selected for death, he would be transported by bus from the institution where he lived—usually along with several dozen others in the same predicament—to the closest T4 institution. The side windows of the buses were painted over in a vain attempt to conceal this activity. Once the victims arrived at the T4 center, they were instructed to disrobe. In some cases they were then brought before a physician who briefly interviewed them, and in rare cases, one or more might be exempted from the death sentence and returned to their home institution. Most patients, however, were led naked into the gas chambers, where they perished.

Many of the victims understood their impending fate. One of the nurses in charge of ten-year-old children at the Kalmenhof-Idstein state hospital reported, "Everyone talked about it, even the children talked about it. They were all afraid to go to the hospital. They were fearful that they would not come back. It was a general rumor. The children played a coffin game. We were astonished that the children understood." A boy at the same asylum who had partial paralysis, but no mental problems whatsoever, called his parents in April 1941, asking them to bring him home. He told them that he was going to be transferred, and he knew that meant death. His parents called this institution and were reassured that this would not happen, but when the father arrived the next day to see his son, he had already been sent to Hadamar to die. Some patients wrote letters to their families, indicating that they were soon going to die. Others rebuked the T4 perpetrators. One female patient confronted some T4 physicians, asking, "Well, are you again looking for new victims, you mass murderers?"[28]

Families were only notified after their loved ones were removed from their home institutions. Then they received a form letter telling them that it had been necessary to transfer their family member to another facility. Soon T4 personnel would send them a deceitful notification that their loved one had arrived safely at the other facility. Shortly thereafter, they would receive another letter, informing them that their family member was dead. These letters were filled with misinformation, including a fake cause of death, falsified location of death, and counterfeit signatures. Mirroring the euthanasia mindset of the perpetrators, the letters also asserted the following or a similar message: "With the incurable mental illness of the one who died, death is a deliverance for her."[29]

The mass killing operation ran smoothly, efficiently murdering dozens of people every weekday. However, the T4 program encountered a problem. Despite their best efforts, they could not keep the program a secret for long. Residents of the cities with T4 institutions began noticing that buses were arriving daily at these facilities with many patients, but leaving empty. A while after the patients arrived, plumes of acrid smoke—which smelled strangely like burnt flesh—rose from the chimneys for all to see. It did not take a genius to figure out what was going on. Even the children in these cities knew—in Hadamar children began nicknaming these buses "murder crates." Further, administrators of institutions for disabled people, some of them run by the churches, began to notice that the patients transferred to these facilities were dying immediately upon arrival. Also, sometimes the fake cause of death listed on the death certificate raised eyebrows, such as the patients who allegedly died of appendicitis, even though their appendixes had been removed earlier in life.

While attempting to avoid unpopularity by keeping the euthanasia program as secret as possible, the Nazi regime tried to win over the public to its pro-euthanasia position. It had already produced several documentaries that dehumanized people with disabilities, but in 1941 Nazi propagandists cleverly produced a full-length feature film that creatively explored the issue of euthanasia. *Ich klage an* (*I Accuse*) told the fictional tale of a lovely, talented woman who developed multiple sclerosis. Not wanting to live with this debilitating condition, the woman asks her physician to provide her with medication to end her life. He refuses, but the lady's husband, who is also a physician, complies with her wishes and assists her in committing suicide. The husband is then put on trial for his illegal deed, but he ably defends himself, contending that his action was good and noble. He is portrayed in the film as a hero, idealistically fighting against an archaic law. Of course, the film was not really featuring a situation analogous to the Nazi euthanasia program, because the victims of the Nazi program were not asking to die. The Nazi program was involuntary euthanasia (and on a massive scale), but the film's scenario involved assisted suicide or voluntary euthanasia of an individual. Though we have no way to gauge its impact on the thinking of Germans, the film was extremely popular, and over fifteen million Germans viewed it by the end of the war.[30]

German Opposition to the Nazi Euthanasia Program

Some, however, were not moved by the film. As early as the summer of 1940, opposition to the Nazi euthanasia program had begun to stir, though most of it was not expressed publicly. The Protestant pastor Paul Gerhard Braune, who directed a Protestant asylum, and the Catholic Cardinal Adolf Bertram wrote letters to Hitler protesting the killing. Other church leaders, Protestant and Catholic, wrote to the Minister of Justice and other Nazi officials to voice opposition. Also in the summer of 1940, Lothar Kreyssig, a German judge who learned about the T4 operation, alerted the Minister of Justice about the patently illegal activities. Kreyssig followed this up by filing murder charges against Bouhler. However, the Nazi Minister of Justice soon forced Kreyssig to withdraw the accusations and to resign from his judicial post.[31]

Local unrest over the killings in the T4 institutions also mounted, causing Nazi officials to shut down the killing operations at Brandenburg in September 1940 and at Grafeneck in December 1940. Closing these two facilities did not significantly slow down the killing, however, because the administrators simply transferred the mass murder to new sites, opening up new T4 facilities at Bernburg to replace Brandenburg and at Hadamar to replace Grafeneck. Thus four T4 institutions continued gassing victims relentlessly in late 1940 and early 1941.

Until the summer of 1941 the Nazis were able to keep a lid on public protests against the euthanasia program. They jailed Pastor Braune in August 1940 for three months, and other objectors recognized that they might face similar treatment if they spoke out publicly. Nevertheless, on August 3, 1941, Catholic Bishop von Galen of Münster boldly preached a sermon explicitly criticizing the Nazi euthanasia program. Six days earlier he had written to the state prosecutor in Münster, alleging that an operation was being planned to remove and murder patients from a mental asylum near Münster. He received no response, so he decided it was time to go public. Galen informed his audience that the Nazi government was killing people with disabilities, and he reminded his audience that these murders were still illegal and should be prosecuted.[32] Galen's printed sermon was quickly banned by the Nazi regime, so it had to be distributed surreptitiously, since anyone caught circulating it risked punishment. However, British officials soon obtained a copy of this sermon—together with a couple of Galen's other sermons criticizing the Nazi regime. The British pounced on them as a propaganda tool, reading them on the BBC and even airdropping them on German cities.

Hitler was furious at Galen's audacity, but he refrained from taking action against the popular bishop. Hitler told his entourage that he did not want to make a martyr out of Galen by imprisoning him. However, he also promised that after the war he would settle scores with Galen. He ominously declared, "The bishop of Münster will yet stand before the firing squad."[33]

Decentralizing the Euthanasia Program

On August 24, just three weeks after Galen's sermon, Hitler ordered that the T4 facilities that were still functioning—Hartheim, Sonnenstein, Bernburg, and Hadamar—cease their killing operations. (Later, however, some of these would reactivate their gas chambers to kill sick concentration camp inmates or forced laborers). By this time medical personnel at the T4 institutions had murdered about 70,000 disabled individuals. It seems that Hitler closed the T4 facilities when they were in full swing, because he was sensitive to the growing unpopularity of the euthanasia program. Galen's sermon was probably just the last straw, since it gave wider publicity to the clandestine program that was no longer all that secret.

The order to cease euthanasia operations at the T4 facilities, however, was by no means the end of the Nazi euthanasia program, for Hitler was determined to continue killing people with disabilities. He simply instructed Brandt, Bouhler, and other leaders in the euthanasia program to decentralize the killing and mask it more effectively. They now transferred the killing to many institutions and instead of gas chambers, they used lethal injections, poisonous tablets, and starvation as their preferred methods. This decentralized process did slow down the killing somewhat after August 1941, but the Nazis still managed to kill another 130,000 disabled Germans before the end of World War II.

Whether it was intended or not, one advantage—from the Nazi standpoint—of closing the T4 facilities was that the personnel could be transferred east to participate in another barbarous mass murder even grander in scale—the mass killing of Jews. Many personnel from the T4 program helped establish or played leading roles in the newly created death camps. The physician Irmfried Eberl, for instance, who directed the T4 centers in Brandenburg and later in Bernburg, became the first commandant of the Treblinka death camp. The first commandant of the Sobibor death camp was another T4 operative, Franz Stangl, who later replaced Eberl at Treblinka. All told, at least ninety personnel from the T4 program worked in death camps at Belzec, Sobibor, and Treblinka.[34] At these camps they killed Jews using the same methods they had refined in the T4 centers: pumping carbon monoxide gas into sealed gas chambers and then incinerating the bodies.

Aftermath of the Nazi Euthanasia Program

Germany's defeat in 1945 brought an end to their euthanasia program. Bouhler committed suicide after being arrested in May 1945.

In 1946–47 American prosecutors and judges put twenty physicians (including Karl Brandt) and three government officials (including Viktor Brack) on trial for their crimes, especially for the euthanasia program (some were on trial for conducting barbarous medical experiments as well). This was known as the Nuremberg Physicians' Trial or the Doctors' Trial, though its official name was United States of America v. Karl Brandt, et al. Brandt and Brack were condemned to death by hanging, which was carried out in 1948.[35]

Paul Nitsche also was condemned to death in a separate trial and executed in 1948 by guillotine. Dr. Heyde took a fake identity and continued to practice medicine in West Germany, until being discovered in 1959. He committed suicide shortly before his trial in 1964.

However, not all of the attitudes motivating the Nazi euthanasia program perished with the regime. Some of the personnel were able to cover up their crimes sufficiently to avoid prosecution, and some continued practicing medicine in post-war Germany. The most spectacular and notorious example of this was Werner Catel, the physician Richard Kretschmar had approached about killing his baby.

As the physician in charge of the Kretschmar infant, Catel was involved in the Nazi euthanasia program from the very start, after Brandt authorized this infant's death. Then he became one of the three physicians leading the child euthanasia program. During this period Catel was professor of pediatrics at the University of Leipzig. His main role in the child euthanasia program was to examine the forms detailing the hereditary illnesses of infants and decide—together with two other physicians—whether the infants should be put to death. He also set up a ward at his university hospital to kill such infants from his region.[36]

After World War II Catel was able to cover up his crimes sufficiently to be exonerated by a denazification tribunal. He continued practicing medicine, and in 1954 became professor of pediatric medicine at the University of Kiel. However, information about his involvement in the Nazi child euthanasia program surfaced, resulting in his retirement in 1960.

Catel aroused more controversy a couple of years later, when he published a book suggesting that Germany should begin practicing euthanasia once again. Germany's leading news magazine, *Der Spiegel*, interviewed Catel in 1964 about his views on euthanasia. Catel denied that his proposal bore any resemblance to the Nazi program, but he defended involuntary euthanasia for infants, when physicians determine that a baby is a "soulless being." How this proposal differed substantially from what Catel was doing in the child euthanasia program in the early 1940s is unclear.[37]

A Clear Warning

The revelations that came out at the Nuremberg Physicians' Trial about the Nazi mass murder of disabled people, along with other related revelations, generally evoked revulsion against euthanasia both in Germany and elsewhere. There could surely be no clearer example of the ease with which "mercy killing" can be wielded against those with no wish to die.

Thus, in the post-war era, a new generation of German physicians were trained to uphold the individual rights of patients. Sensitivity to the Nazi past helped keep the German medical community wary of the dangers of euthanasia—at least, as we shall see, for a time.

6. Since 1960: Europe Reopens Death's Door

A NN G. WAS A FORTY-FOUR-YEAR-OLD BELGIAN WOMAN WHO suffered mental distress linked to anorexia nervosa, an eating disorder. She consulted one of the leading experts on anorexia nervosa, the Belgian psychiatrist Walter Vandereycken. But instead of helping to alleviate her suffering, Vandereycken compounded it by sexually abusing her. In 2012 Ann appeared on a Belgian TV show, accusing Vandereycken of having sexual relations with her and with multiple other patients. Vandereycken publicly admitted that this was true.

A few months later, Ann was dead. In a cruel irony, another psychiatrist—instead of easing the suffering that had been exacerbated by a fellow psychiatrist—approved Ann's request for euthanasia. In doing so he also prevented her from testifying against her abuser, in what was called by some a clear conflict of interest.[1]

This case highlights the murkiness surrounding so-called voluntary euthanasia, even setting aside the issue of the sanctity of life. Does a traumatized person have the clarity of mind to assess her own chances of recovery? Does a medical degree confer integrity?

And yet in the past few decades, more and more European countries—led by the Netherlands and Belgium—have begun legalizing euthanasia.

What has driven the shift toward legalization? Two interrelated developments in the last half of the twentieth century made euthanasia and assisted suicide more acceptable to some Europeans.[2] First, we have seen the increasing secularization of society. Christian churches, especially the Roman Catholic Church, have been and still are some of the strongest opponents of euthanasia and assisted suicide. The decreasing influence of these churches—not only as institutions, but also in their intellectual impact—has led to a decline in belief in the sanctity of human life. This has significantly reduced the opposition to euthanasia and assisted suicide.

Second, from the 1960s on there has been a related shift toward personal autonomy. This emphasis on "what I want" has resulted in the legalization of abortion and the relaxation of divorce laws, and has encouraged greater openness to the idea of euthanasia and assisted suicide.

The Netherlands's Path to Legalizing Euthanasia

A poll in 1950 indicated that 54 percent of people in the Netherlands opposed legalizing euthanasia. However, by 1991, only about 10 percent of the Dutch population opposed euthanasia completely.[3] Further, whereas physicians in many countries have resisted euthanasia, in the Netherlands the medical profession helped pave the way toward legalizing euthanasia.

This change in Dutch attitudes about euthanasia accompanied the increased secularization of Dutch society. Indeed, secularization was much more rapid in the Netherlands than in most other western European countries. For instance, in 1987 only 46 percent of the population in the Netherlands was affiliated with a church, while in the UK 76 percent still had some kind of church membership.[4] Probably in part because of this increased secularization, Dutch society, according to John Griffiths, "transformed itself into a hotbed of social and cultural experimentation" as it embraced the Sexual Revolution, abortion, and drug use.[5]

Legal Cases

Until the 1970s euthanasia was not a significant topic of public discussion in the Netherlands. This changed in 1971, when a seventy-eight-year-old deaf and partly paralyzed woman asked her daughter to end her life. The daughter, Geertruida Postma, was a physician. She complied by giving her mother a lethal injection. Since euthanasia and assisted suicide were illegal in the Netherlands, Postma was prosecuted, and her 1973 trial inflamed public debate over the issue. She was convicted, but only received a one-week suspended sentence.[6] The controversy over Postma's trial led that same year to the formation of the Dutch Association for Voluntary Euthanasia (often translated less literally as the Dutch Right to Die Society), which began promoting legalization of euthanasia. Its motto is "A dignified life deserves a dignified death."[7]

Despite the leniency shown toward the perpetrator in the *Postma* case, the legal status of euthanasia and assisted suicide in the Netherlands did not change substantially at that time. However, a high-profile court case in 1981, the *Wertheim* case, would bring significant changes to the way that euthanasia and assisted suicide were treated by Dutch courts. This case involved an isolated, alcoholic woman who believed she had cancer (she did not), who asked Corry Wertheim-Elink Schuurman, a voluntary euthanasia activist, to provide her with a lethal drug.

In the *Wertheim* decision the court did not technically abolish the law prohibiting euthanasia and assisted suicide, but it ruled that as long as certain conditions were met, assisted suicide should not be prosecuted. It stipulated that assisted suicide could be carried out if the patient was suffering unbearably, if the decision to die was both voluntary and persistent, if the patient was informed of other alternatives, if there were no alternatives to improve the patient's condition, and if the patient's death did not inflict suffering on others.

Remarkably, the court did not insist that the patient had to have a terminal illness (indeed the person Wertheim had euthanized was not terminally ill, but was suffering and had requested help in dying). The court further required that it could only be done by a physician who had consulted a second physician.[8] Wertheim had not followed these guidelines, so she was convicted. However, as in the *Postma* case, she only received a suspended sentence.

The first court case in the Netherlands in which a physician was fully acquitted for killing a patient at the patient's request came in the 1983–84 *Schoonheim* case. This case concerned a physician who had euthanized a ninety-five-year-old bedridden patient, who was not suffering from a terminal illness. The patient repeatedly expressed a desire to die, and the physician, after consulting another physician, accommodated her request. In this case, the Dutch Supreme Court ruled that a physician could legally argue that euthanasia is an act of "necessity," i.e., an act which one is unable to avoid and thus is not liable to prosecution.[9] This case made clear that the Dutch courts were allowing euthanasia, even for non-terminal conditions.

"Normal Medical Practice"

In the 1980s the Royal Dutch Medical Association was divided on the issue of euthanasia. It appointed a committee in 1984, which recommended that the association take a neutral stance on euthanasia. However, the committee also insisted that if euthanasia were permitted, it should be performed solely by physicians. The full association accepted the committee's recommendation.[10]

By the 1990s, it was clear that assisted suicide and euthanasia were officially tolerated by the Dutch judicial system. In the years 1981 to 1997, twenty physicians were prosecuted for practicing euthanasia. Eleven cases ended in acquittal; in three cases the physicians were convicted but received no sentence; and in six cases the physicians were convicted but given suspended sentences. No physician was actually punished for killing a patient, even though Dutch law still technically forbade euthanasia.[11] Thus, by 1990 many Dutch physicians were regularly practicing euthanasia. That year about 2,700 patients—about 1.9 percent of the total deaths in the Netherlands—were killed at their own request.[12]

In 1990 the Dutch government appointed the Remmelink Committee to investigate end-of-life decisions and statistics related to end-of-life care, including euthanasia and assisted suicide. In its 1991 report it divulged that 54 percent of physicians surveyed had performed euthanasia, and 34 percent more considered it conceivable that they would do so in the future. Only 12 percent of physicians indicated they were opposed to killing their patients, but of these, two-thirds were willing to refer the patient to another physician to do so.[13] The Remmelink Committee affirmed that euthanasia was by that time "normal medical practice."[14]

Why Do the Dutch Want to Die?

What was motivating so many Dutch patients to request euthanasia or assisted suicide (and most were requesting euthanasia rather than assisted suicide)? Some may find this surprising, but pain was not the primary reason for wanting to die. In a 1990 study only 46 percent of those asking for euthanasia listed pain as a reason for their request. A more important factor, listed by 57 percent of respondents, was loss of dignity, and 46 percent mentioned the related notion of unworthy dying. Being dependent on others influenced the decision of 33 percent of those requesting euthanasia, and 23 percent mentioned tiredness of life as a motivation for wanting to die. (These percentages total far more than 100 percent, because many people listed multiple reasons for wanting to die, not just one.)

Most Dutch men and women requesting euthanasia are in the final stages of life. Many are within days or weeks of death, and a 1995 survey suggested that only 9 percent of those euthanized would have lived more than one month.[15] However, Dutch courts did not insist that a person be in the last stage of life. Indeed, in the 1994 *Chabot* case, the Dutch Supreme Court ruled that it was permissible to euthanize patients with psychiatric illnesses who had no physical illness at all. The court claimed that psychiatric patients could be considered competent to consent to euthanasia.[16]

Making Common Practice Legal

Finally, in 2001 the Dutch parliament passed a euthanasia law that legislated what the courts had already decided and what Dutch physicians were already practicing. Indeed, by that time 2.8 percent of deaths in the Netherlands were brought about by voluntary euthanasia or assisted suicide.

The new law, which went into effect in 2002, stipulated that only physicians can participate in euthanasia and assisted suicide, and they must respect certain restrictions. Specifically, it required that the physician: "a. holds the conviction that the request by the patient was voluntary and well-considered, b. holds the conviction that the patient's suffering was lasting and unbearable, c. has informed the patient about the situation he was in and about his prospects, d. the patient hold[s] the conviction that there was no other reasonable solution for the situation he was in, e. has consulted at least one other, independent physician who has seen the patient and has given his written opinion on the requirements of due care, referred to in parts a-d, and f. has terminated the life or assisted in suicide with due care."[17]

This law permitted euthanasia for patients sixteen to eighteen years old, as long as parents are informed, and for patients twelve to sixteen years old, if parents consented.[18] Physicians were not obligated to offer euthanasia to patients. If they did euthanize a patient, however, they were required to report it to one of the five Regional Review Committees established by the Dutch government.[19]

Since 2001, euthanasia deaths in the Netherlands have continued to increase. Dutch physicians reported that in 2019 there were 6,361 deaths by euthanasia or assisted suicide (mostly by euthanasia), which represented about 4.2 percent of the total deaths in the Netherlands.[20]

Despite the stipulations in the 2001 law, courts have been remarkably lax about enforcing the safeguards. For instance, in 2015 a Dutch appeals court acquitted Albert Heringa, who had helped his mother commit suicide in 2008. His mother was ninety-nine years old, blind, and wanted to die, even though she had no other serious illness. According to the law, only physicians can legally assist in suicides, and Heringa was not a physician. Nor had he complied with other restrictions in the 2001 law, which include consultation with a second physician. Indeed, his mother's physician had refused to help her commit suicide. Heringa gave his mother a drug overdose and filmed his actions. In 2010 a Dutch TV station aired his film in a documentary.[21]

The Power of the Physician

A 2016 euthanasia case resulted in the first prosecution of a physician for performing euthanasia after the 2001 law. In that case, Marinou Arends, a Dutch geriatrician, administered a fatal injection to a lady suffering from dementia who told Arends three times that she *did not* want to be killed. Even after Arends drugged the woman's coffee to make her compliant, she struggled against the fatal injection. Family members present had to restrain her so Arends could give the injection.

The reason Arends killed her was that the lady had given an advance directive that asked for euthanasia if she became demented. Arends believed she was following the true wishes of the lady, even though at the time of the injection, the lady clearly stated three times that she did not want to die yet. Even though the regional review board ruled that Arends's actions were inappropriate, she was ultimately acquitted in 2020.[22]

The case illustrates only one of a host of issues regarding the question of who holds the power of life and death. Though patients in the Netherlands have to request euthanasia or assisted suicide, physicians make the ultimate determination. They can say yes, or they can say no.[23] They can—as Arends did—overrule the current wishes of the patient in favor of the patient's past wishes.

Some critics of euthanasia have pointed out the irony in this: One of the strongest arguments advanced for euthanasia is personal autonomy, and one of the motivations giving impetus to euthanasia is the fear of the expanding power of the medical profession to extend lives. People don't want to be forced to live beyond natural limits.

In 2015 over 12,000 patients requested euthanasia, but only 55 percent of these requests were approved. However, Dutch physicians are not resistant to outside pressure. A 2019 study of Dutch physicians' attitudes about euthanasia found that over 44 percent of Dutch physicians reported that they felt pressured by society to offer euthanasia. When they refused specific euthanasia requests, 60 percent claimed they felt pressured by the patient and 31 percent felt pressured by relatives of the patient to approve the request.[24] These findings should come as an unpleasant surprise to those naïve enough to place complete trust in physicians—who are, as should be obvious, as fallible and easily swayed, as open to corruption and confusion, as other humans.

Psychiatric Patients

One of the most controversial features of euthanasia in the Netherlands is granting euthanasia to psychiatric patients who are not suffering any physical illness. Many of these patients have attempted suicide in the past, before requesting euthanasia to end their mental torment. In 2011–14 the Netherlands reported 110 cases of euthanasia for psychiatric problems. Of these, sixty-six cases were published on a government website. Most of the patients had personality disorders and were described as socially isolated and lonely. Many suffered from depression. One case reported, "The patient indicated that she had had a life without love and therefore had no right to exist." Another case stated, "The patient was an utterly lonely man whose life had been a failure." In 24 percent of the cases, physicians disagreed about whether euthanasia should be allowed.[25]

By 2014 half of the patients euthanized for psychiatric problems had to appeal to the Dutch End-of-Life Clinic, because their physicians refused to approve their request. The End-of-Life Clinic was founded in 2012 with the support of the Dutch Association for Voluntary Euthanasia to provide euthanasia for Dutch patients in cases where their physicians did not offer euthanasia or denied their request. In 2019 the End-of-Life Clinic changed its name to the Euthanasia Expertise Center. Its network of mobile physicians are avid proponents of euthanasia who consult with patients and then provide euthanasia at the patients' homes.[26] The year 2019 saw sixty-eight psychiatric patients euthanized in the Netherlands, and fifty-two of those cases were handled by the Euthanasia Expertise Center.[27]

Killing: Easier than Caring

The 2019 annual report of the Regional Euthanasia Review Committees in the Netherlands claims "that due care is exercised in the practice of euthanasia in the Netherlands," because in only four of the

6,361 cases of euthanasia and assisted suicide reported that year did the physicians fail to follow proper procedures.

However, that report also shows how the pro-euthanasia mentality in the Netherlands has expanded euthanasia to people suffering from many conditions, including those without any physical pain.

In addition to the sixty-eight psychiatric patients killed, another 162 patients were euthanized for dementia. Most of these were in early phases of dementia and feared their future prospects, but two were in advanced stages of dementia and were euthanized based on advance directives. Some of these advance directives seem vague and subject to the interpretation of the physicians as to what they think constitutes a worthwhile or dignified life. For instance, one advance directive that permitted the euthanasia of a man in his seventies stated, "If, for any reason, I end up in a mental or physical state that offers no real prospect of returning to a reasonable and dignified life, I do not wish to continue living and wish to die quickly and peacefully." In another case a man in his 50s went blind, and this distressed him so badly that even though he had no other serious physical or mental problem, he was granted euthanasia. The report stated, "The knowledge that he would eventually become completely blind and hence dependent on other people and various aids distressed him. He did not want that. He was adamant on this point." Another troubling feature of Dutch euthanasia practice is that married couples—seventeen couples in 2019—are being euthanized simultaneously.[28] Essentially, then, a would-be widow or widower's fear of a lonely future is enough to qualify for euthanasia in the Netherlands. Surely a more human and humane response would be to work towards creating a community where those who are sick, disabled, or grieving find support and companionship.

As things now stand, however, anyone who believes that he or she is suffering unbearably—no matter what the physical, psychiatric, or emotional problem may be—may request euthanasia from his or her physician. The vast majority opt for euthanasia rather than assisted suicide. Most have a terminal illness, but this is not required, and many are euthanized without a terminal illness. Indeed, some have no physical illness at all and would likely live for decades longer. Thus, many Dutch patients who are euthanized are not suffering any kind of physical pain, but are experiencing existential suffering caused by loneliness, lack of social interaction, and a sense of meaninglessness.

If their physician agrees that they are experiencing unbearable suffering with no hope of recovery, as physicians do in the majority of such cases in the Netherlands, then the patients may be euthanized. If the physician does not agree, sometimes the patient consults the Euthanasia Expertise Center, who may step in to euthanize the patient. Currently over five percent of deaths in the Netherlands are either euthanasia or assisted suicide, and this number has been increasing over the years since full legalization in 2002.

Belgium Follows Suit

Belgium was heavily influenced by the Dutch relaxation of anti-euthanasia laws.

In 1980 two pro-euthanasia organizations were founded in Belgium, one for Dutch speakers and the other for French speakers. At the time there was little sympathy for euthanasia in Belgium, and these organizations were considered radical. But Belgians' attitudes about euthanasia began to change, particularly in Flanders (the northern, Dutch-speaking part of Belgium), where people closely followed the developments in the neighboring Netherlands.

A survey in 1998 found that 1.3 percent of deaths in Flanders were by euthanasia or physician-assisted suicide, even though it was still illegal. Unlike in the Netherlands, prosecutors in Belgium never prosecuted anyone for euthanasia or assisted suicide. Thus its legal status was far murkier than in the Netherlands, where courts had stipulated that if certain guidelines were followed, physicians could euthanize patients with impunity. By 2000 about three-fourths of all Belgians supported the legalization of euthanasia.[29]

Path to Legalization

The June 1999 Belgian elections were pivotal in legalizing euthanasia because the Christian Democratic Party, which had been the ruling party in Belgium for over four decades, suffered defeat. A coalition of liberal, socialist, and green parties formed the new government, and they favored legalization of euthanasia.

In May 2002 the Belgian parliament passed a law permitting voluntary euthanasia, which went into effect in September. Belgium was thus only a few months behind the Netherlands in legalizing euthanasia.

Unsurprisingly, Belgium's euthanasia law was very similar to the Dutch law. The Belgian law requires that the patient must be in a "medically futile condition of constant and unbearable physical or mental suffering that cannot be alleviated, resulting from a serious and incurable disorder caused by illness or accident." The patient must voluntarily request euthanasia, and the physician must consult with another physician before administering the fatal injection.[30]

However, in 2015 the Belgian Constitutional Court ruled that it is legitimate for a physician to euthanize a patient, even if the consulting physician(s) gave a negative report. Thus the consulting physicians' decision has no real clout, even when the consulting physician is a psychiatrist in a psychiatric case. Indeed a 2011 article showed that four out of 363 euthanasia deaths examined in that study were carried out despite negative advice from the consulting physician.[31]

For Any and Every Reason

As in the Netherlands, the Belgian law does not require that the person seeking euthanasia must have a terminal illness or be suffering any physical pain. In 2013 the ninety-five-year-old Belgian Nobel Prize-winning scientist Christian de Duve died from euthanasia, even though he had no serious illness threatening his life. His decision to seek euthanasia came after he fell in his home and felt helpless. Apparently, his family and society in general not only did not try to dissuade him from taking this step, but many encouraged him to do it, calling it honorable and lauding him as brave.[32]

A person suffering purely from psychological problems can also be euthanized in Belgium, as in Ann G.'s case, discussed at the top of this chapter. Another tragic example of this was Nancy Verhelst, whose parents rejected her because she was a girl and they wanted a boy. She had three brothers and always felt inferior to them. As an adult she tried to deal with the psychological problems caused by her parents' rejection by deciding to become a man, changing her name to Nathan and undergoing sex-change operations. However, she was so disgusted by the results of the operations that she asked for euthanasia to put an end to her psychological torment. In 2013, at age forty-four, she was granted her request for euthanasia at a Brussels hospital.

Verhelst was not alone; the previous year fifty-two Belgians were euthanized because they were experiencing psychological distress.[33] One might think that euthanasia in most psychiatric cases would be substantially delayed, as physicians and psychiatrists worked to dissuade the patient from taking this step. But in about 60 percent of the euthanasia deaths for psychiatric conditions in 2016–17, the time from the request for euthanasia to the death of the patient was three months or less.[34]

Policing Themselves

To verify that Belgian physicians follow proper protocol and do not abuse their power over life and death, the Belgian government established the Federal Commission for Euthanasia Control and Evaluation. This commission has sixteen members, eight of whom must be physicians. Many of these physicians offer euthanasia to their patients. The commission is headed by one of the most passionate proponents of euthanasia, Wim Distelmans, an oncologist and medical professor in Brussels who has probably killed more patients than any other physician in Belgium (and possibly anywhere else in the world). Because Distelmans and other members of the commission participate in euthanasia, to some extent they are policing themselves.[35]

In a scholarly article on Belgian euthanasia, Klaus Raus and some colleagues explained that the commission reviews all its cases anonymously, unless they suspect problems, so members of the commission could be reviewing their own cases without other members of the commission even knowing it. Because of this, Raus concluded, "Furthermore, due to the Commission's composition and the authority it has taken upon itself, it might actually function as a shield, rather than a monitoring body."[36] In its first eighteen years the only case the commission referred to the public prosecutor was one that was highly public, because the participants not only flouted the rules, but also sought attention by being filmed and televised.[37]

The effectiveness of the Federal Commission for Euthanasia Control and Evaluation is questionable in another regard: studies have shown that physicians do not report all cases of euthanasia. This is especially the case when the physicians have not followed all the proper protocols. In 2013, for instance, a study showed that 7.4 percent of euthanasia deaths were done without consulting another physician. However, the Federal Commission for Euthanasia Control and Evaluation reported that year that 100 percent of reported cases had a consulting physician. Quite obviously, some cases were not being reported, and the Federal Commission has no way of finding out, because it has no investigatory powers. It only examines the reports submitted. Indeed a 2018 study suggested that one-third of all euthanasia cases in Belgium are not reported to the commission.[38]

Widening the Net

Distelmans, the leader of the Belgian commission, has been a tireless promoter of the legalization and expansion of euthanasia. He promoted the legalization of euthanasia for minors before 2014, when the Belgian parliament legalized it. In order to qualify for euthanasia, minors must be conscious and capable of making a voluntary judgment (and a psychiatrist must verify this). Parents must also consent. Unlike adults, minors must be suffering some kind of terminal illness in order to be euthanized. In 2016–17 three minors—ages 9, 11, and 17—were legally killed by their physicians.

Since its legalization in 2002 the numbers and scope of euthanasia have been increasing. In 2019 there were 2,656 euthanasia deaths in Belgium, which was 2.4 percent of the total deaths that year. In Flanders the percentage was much higher: 4.6 percent.

Well over half (62 percent) of Belgium's euthanasia deaths in 2018–19 were for patients with terminal cancer. However, the diagnosis of 17.4 percent of euthanasia deaths those years was "poly-pathology," a category increasingly used by elderly patients who are "tired of life" and have multiple chronic problems. Indeed a health law professor, Herman Nys, has publicly stated that poly-pathology is a legitimate reason to grant euthanasia to those who are "tired of life." Of the non-terminal euthanasia cases in 2018–19, 47 percent were diagnosed with poly-pathology.

One problem with this designation is that patients with both a psychiatric problem and some other physical ailment may be listed as suffering from poly-pathology. The attending physician could then evade the need to consult with a psychiatrist, because the Belgian commission overseeing euthanasia has determined that general practitioners can diagnose and adjudicate poly-pathology without consulting specialists for each condition.[39]

Switzerland

The historical development and current practice of assisted suicide in Switzerland is radically different from that of the Netherlands and Belgium. The most obvious difference is that in Switzerland euthanasia is still illegal, even though a majority of Swiss citizens favor its legalization. Assisted suicide has a more complicated status.

Legalities, or Lack Thereof

While the Netherlands and Belgium were moving to legalize euthanasia, advocates for euthanasia and assisted suicide in Switzerland were taking advantage of the Swiss legal code of 1937, which did not ban assisted suicide unless it was committed for selfish motives (such as getting an inheritance sooner). Switzerland has no law regulating assisted suicide other than this.

Thus no law clarifies who is eligible for assisted suicide, nor is there any requirement for consultation. Activists have taken advantage of the absence of laws against assisted suicide to set up assisted suicide programs and clinics, not only for Swiss citizens, but also (as we shall see) for suicide tourists.

Also, assisted suicide in Switzerland is handled by non-medical personnel, so physicians are normally not as intimately involved in the deaths. To be sure, if the person committing suicide wants to use a lethal drug (as is most often the case), Swiss physicians have to prescribe it (usually pentobarbital). However, the person requesting it generally has to take it with the help of a volunteer from Exit or Dignitas, and usually these are not medical professionals.

Exit

In 1982 two organizations promoting assisted suicide formed, one for the German-speaking parts of Switzerland, and the other for the French-speaking areas. Both were named Exit. The Swiss German Exit offered its services in assisting suicide to those who had "poor prognosis, unbearable suffering or unreasonable disability." The Swiss French Exit had similar provisions.[40] During its first ten years of operation the German Swiss Exit sent a suicide manual to all members over eighteen years of age who had been members for over three years. It provided detailed explanations about how to kill oneself with a plastic bag or with drugs.[41] By 2007 this organization had 50,000 members and twenty-one volunteers to assist in suicides. That year, in their zeal to facilitate suicide, these volunteers managed 23 percent of the time to assist in suicides within seven days of their first contact with a person requesting their help.[42]

This enthusiasm for death has spread to the general public. A survey of Swiss citizens over 55 years old showed that over 80 percent of them support the legality of assisted suicide, and over 60 percent said they would consider it under some circumstances. Almost 5 percent were already members of a right-to-die society, such as Exit.[43] Unsurprisingly, assisted suicides have been steadily increasing in Switzerland over the past few decades. In 2003, 187 Swiss citizens died from assisted suicide; by 2016 that number had escalated to 928 deaths,[44] accounting for 1.4 percent of all the deaths in Switzerland.[45]

Suicide Tourism

One of the more controversial aspects of Swiss assisted suicide is the emergence of suicide tourism. In 1998 the organization Dignitas formed to extend assisted suicide to foreigners, who would come to

Switzerland to die. At the end of 2020 Dignitas had over 10,000 members from many different countries and that year participated in 221 assisted suicides.[46]

Because the Swiss constitutional court ruled in 2006 that mental illness is an acceptable cause for physicians to prescribe a lethal medication, Swiss suicide tourists only need to plead psychological distress.[47] One of the more bizarre cases of suicide tourism was an 85-year-old woman from Italy, Oriella Cazzanello, who was physically healthy, but felt "weighed down by ageing and the inevitable loss of the looks of which she was proud." Unbeknownst to her family, in 2014 she flew to Basel, Switzerland, where a suicide clinic helped her end her life. Her family was shocked and dismayed when they received news of her demise.[48]

Elsewhere in Europe

Euthanasia and assisted suicide are still illegal in most European countries. A survey in 2008 indicated that Denmark, Belgium, France, the Netherlands, and Sweden had the highest public acceptance of euthanasia. Less public acceptance was found in Greece, Ireland, Northern Ireland, and Austria; and the least support was found in Kosovo, Cyprus, Turkey, Georgia, and Armenia.[49]

Austria attempted to ban assisted suicide, but an Austrian court in December 2020 struck down Austria's ban as unconstitutional, though it delayed implementation until December 2021 to allow parliament time to pass legislation regulating assisted suicide.[50]

In March 2021 the Spanish parliament passed a law legalizing euthanasia.

As for France, a 2007 poll found that 87 percent of the French public approve of euthanasia. The French medical profession, however, is not as supportive.[51] French President Emmanuel Macron favors legalization of euthanasia, though as of early 2024 he had not been able to achieve this.[52]

Despite the pro-death push in the UK during the 1930s to 1950s, when the UK decriminalized suicide in 1961, the new law expressly forbade assisted suicide. Some segments of British society remain sympathetic to assisted suicide, however. In 1968 the British Humanist Association, the National Council for Civil Liberties, and the National Secular Society all passed resolutions affirming support for voluntary euthanasia. Bills to legalize euthanasia have been introduced into parliament five times between 1950 and 1994, but all five have failed. In 2005 a survey in the UK showed that over 70 percent of the British public favored euthanasia for those with terminal illnesses.[53]

At this time, however, euthanasia and assisted suicide are still illegal in the UK.

Why is this so? Religious faith in the UK has declined, so it seems unlikely that sanctity-of-life beliefs are responsible.

In his sympathetic study of the history of the British euthanasia movement, Nick Kemp argues that the refusal to allow euthanasia and assisted suicide in contemporary Britain is largely due to fears of the slippery slope (which we will discuss further in a later chapter). Kemp points out that British euthanasia advocates did not assuage these fears, because many in the movement admitted that they supported euthanasia for non-terminal conditions. Worse, many in the British euthanasia movement supported the legalization of involuntary euthanasia and were promoting voluntary euthanasia as a first step toward that goal.

Kemp seems to share the dehumanizing and inegalitarian attitudes of the more radical euthanasia proponents that he analyzes, stating at the conclusion of his book, "Other individuals while acknowledging that all human life is not of equal worth are unwilling to extinguish promptly a life which is no longer worth living."[54]

This phrase, "a life which is no longer worth living" is hauntingly similar to the phrase frequently used in Nazi Germany to describe people with disabilities: "*lebensunwertes Leben*"—often translated as "life unworthy of life."

And what of Germany? As we have seen, the Nazi euthanasia program that targeted people with disabilities for involuntary euthanasia provided a poignant warning against all such practices. Yet by the 1970s some Germans' attitudes were becoming somewhat more receptive to euthanasia, with several leading German magazines expressing sympathy toward a Dutch physician indicted for euthanizing her mother.[55]

Nevertheless, in response to the pro-death developments in Switzerland, the German parliament passed a law against assisted suicide in 2015. Unfortunately, in February 2020 Germany's Supreme Court ruled that the law against assisted suicide was unconstitutional. Thus assisted suicide (but not euthanasia) is now legal in Germany.[56]

Conclusion

Since the 1960s Europe, especially western Europe, has become more accepting of euthanasia and assisted suicide. European societies have become increasingly secularized, so the Judeo-Christian sanctity-of-life ethic has declined in influence. Journalist Andrew Coyne, commenting on the rising tide of euthanasia, put it starkly: "A society that believes in nothing can offer no argument even against death. A culture that has lost its faith in life cannot comprehend why it should be endured."[57]

7. The United States and Canada Today

IN LATE 2022 CHRISTINE GAUTHIER, A RETIRED CORPORAL, paraplegic, and former Paralympian, testified before a Canadian parliamentary committee that she had been having a long battle with Veterans Affairs Canada to try to get them to install a wheelchair ramp at her home. Without this ramp, she had to crawl to get out of her house. In 2019, when she stressed her dire need for this ramp, a Veterans Affairs case manager replied, "Madam, if you are really so desperate, we can give you medical assistance in dying now."

Gauthier was outraged by this offer of death; she explained, "I was like, 'I can't believe that you will… give me an injection to help me die, but you will not give me the tools I need to help me live. It was really shocking to hear that kind of comment." Even Canadian Prime Minister Justin Trudeau, who is a keen supporter of euthanasia and assisted suicide, was angered by the case manager's response and promised to rein in such abuses.[1]

How did Canada reach this point, where euthanasia and assisted suicide are not only legal and acceptable, but urged on people who simply need basic alterations to their homes? And how did some states in the US come to legalize assisted suicide? It didn't happen overnight.

The US Scene

In 1973 many leading atheists and agnostics, including science writer Isaac Asimov, Nobel Prize-winning biologist Francis Crick, Planned

Parenthood president Alan Guttmacher, behavioral psychologist B. F. Skinner, and bioethicist Joseph Fletcher, signed the Humanist Manifesto II. While this declaration insisted that the "preciousness and dignity of the individual person is a central humanist value," it also affirmed "an individual's right to die with dignity, euthanasia, and the right to suicide."[2]

However, opposition to euthanasia and assisted suicide in the United States was still very strong at that time, especially in Roman Catholic and evangelical Protestant circles. Indeed, some states, such as Missouri in 1984, even passed laws outlawing assisted suicide.

Two developments would gradually create greater acceptance of assisted suicide in the US (though, unlike in the Netherlands, euthanasia would remain taboo). First and probably most importantly, the new cultural attitudes flowing from the sixties would progressively permeate American society, transforming norms in many areas, such as abortion, feminism, and divorce. Gradually American society—like European society before it—became more secular in outlook, moving relentlessly away from traditional Judeo-Christian morality, including its sanctity-of-life ethic.

Second, medical advances and technology altered perceptions about end-of-life medical care, as many people became concerned about protracted deaths in hospitals and the ability of physicians to keep people alive on machines almost indefinitely.

Medical Life Support

The perception that overzealous physicians were trying to keep people alive at all costs, even when their efforts were futile, led to a backlash against such intense medical intervention. Several high-profile cases riveted public attention in the late twentieth and early twenty-first centuries. One of the earliest legal battles involved Karen Ann Quinlan, who in 1975 suffered brain damage and never recovered consciousness. After three months her parents requested that the hospital remove her ventilator, but they refused, so her parents went to court. The New Jersey Supreme Court sided with the parents, so her respirator was disconnected in 1976. However, she continued breathing without the respirator, so with the help of a feeding tube she lived until 1985.[3]

Quinlan's case would give impetus to those wanting to introduce the "living will" into American law. The living will is a document that stipulates what medical intervention a person wants and, more importantly, what medical interventions they would refuse. This document is intended to convey their wishes if their capacity to communicate is impaired in some way, such as by being in a coma. Originally drafted in 1969, the living will was first recognized as a legally binding document in California in 1976. By the end of the twentieth century, nearly all states in the US recognized living wills.[4]

In the 1980s a high-profile case involving end-of-life issues would reach the US Supreme Court. Nancy Cruzan never regained consciousness after an auto accident in 1983. Four years later her parents requested that her feeding and hydration tubes be removed, which would lead, usually within several days or a week, to death by dehydration. The Missouri Supreme Court ruled against the parents in 1988, but the case was appealed to the US Supreme Court. In 1990 the Supreme Court ruled in that case that artificial nutrition and hydration did constitute a medical intervention that competent patients could refuse. Cruzan, however, could not make her wishes known, so they sent the case back to a lower court to determine if Nancy Cruzan would have wanted to refuse treatment. The lower court ruled in the parents' favor, so in December 1990 her feeding and hydration tubes were withdrawn, and she died of dehydration.[5]

"Right to Die" versus "Right to Be Killed"

Even though the Quinlan and Cruzan cases did not involve assisted suicide or active euthanasia, they still gave greater impetus to the right-to-die movement. The Euthanasia Society of America, which was languishing in the early 1960s, would gain greater support by the 1970s as it focused its attention more on refusal of medical life-support than on active euthanasia. Oddly enough, Donald McKinney, who became president of the Euthanasia Society of America in 1965, opposed both assisted suicide and active euthanasia. To reflect this shift in emphasis and to distance itself from the negative connotations of the term "euthanasia," the organization altered its name in 1975, becoming the Society for the Right to Die.[6] When, later, the organization reverted to the promotion of assisted suicide and euthanasia, the concept of "right to die" and "right to be killed" remained grouped in many people's minds.

Indeed, many right-to-die proponents argued forthrightly that refusing medical treatments at the end of one's life was equivalent to euthanasia. These two issues thus became (wrongly) conflated.

The philosopher James Rachels in 1975 published an influential article arguing that the distinction between killing and letting die was illegitimate. Many philosophers who support euthanasia and assisted suicide rely on Rachels's argument. Rachels offered the following make-believe scenario:

> Smith stands to gain a large inheritance if anything should happen to his six-year-old cousin. One evening while the child is taking his bath, Smith sneaks into the bathroom and drowns the child, and then arranges things so that it will look like an accident.
>
> … Jones also stands to gain if anything should happen to his six-year-old cousin. Like Smith, Jones sneaks in planning to drown the child in his bath. However, just as he enters the bathroom Jones sees the child slip and hit his head, and fall face down in the water. Jones is delighted; he stands by, ready to push the child's head back under if it is necessary, but it is not necessary. With only a little thrashing about, the child drowns all by himself, "accidentally," as Jones watches and does nothing.[7]

Rachels claimed that since both men were equally morally culpable, the "killing" versus "letting die" distinction is illegitimate.

But note that in this scenario, both culprits intended the death of the person who died (Rachels comments that they "acted from the same motive" and "had the same end in view when they acted"). Yet in the real-life situations to which this discussion is most relevant—families making difficult decisions over the hospital bed of a terminally ill loved one—the motive is different. Most people who "pull the plug" on a loved one by ending medical treatment are not intending or wanting the death of their loved one. Rather they are accepting the inevitable. The goal in removing medical treatment is not to cause death per se, but simply to not artificially prolong death in a futile attempt to stave it off. Thus to argue, as Rachels does, that ending medical treatment is "the intentional termination of life" is to ignore a crucial distinction. Removing medical treatment for a terminally ill loved one in such cases is not the same as actively killing a person.

The distinction between killing and letting die is enshrined in many law codes, so that a person who does not intervene to help someone who is dying is not legally liable for that person's death. To return to Rachels's example, if a person actively drowns someone, they are legally liable for murder. However, if a bystander sees someone drowning and does not rescue that person, under most law codes, they are not legally liable (even if perhaps they want the person to die).

In 2018 a bizarre case occurred that illustrates this point. Several teens in Florida recorded the cries for help of a drowning man, and instead of rendering assistance, they taunted and ridiculed him as he drowned. This sparked outrage (as well it should). However, the Florida prosecutor admitted that as despicable as their actions were, there was nothing he could charge them with, because refusing to rescue someone in peril is not illegal.[8] Thus, killing is illegal; letting die is not illegal. In this particular case, the action of these teens was clearly immoral, not because they didn't jump in the water to help the man (maybe they couldn't swim or were afraid they would die in the effort to save his life), but because of their hateful attitudes.

This is far removed from situations where family members reluctantly end medical treatment of a terminally ill loved one to allow that person to die. There are many extremely difficult scenarios at the end of people's lives, and it isn't always easy to know when to end treatment and allow a person to die. But the difficulty in making and timing such decisions does not obviate the reality that the intention is love for the person, not a desire to see the person die.

Opponents of assisted suicide and euthanasia have consistently drawn this strict distinction between refusing medical treatment and actively killing a patient or committing suicide. The Catholic Church is one of the staunchest foes of euthanasia and assisted suicide, but already in 1957 Pope Pius XII had issued a statement that affirmed the legitimacy of refusing life-prolonging medical treatments.[9] The Roman Catholic Church continues to recognize this fundamental right of patients, even when such refusal results in death. At the same time, the Roman Catholic Church continues to oppose active measures to end one's life, such as lethal doses of medication.

This is the position held by most opponents of assisted suicide. They recognize the right to refuse treatment and do not consider it to be suicide, assisted suicide, or "passive euthanasia."

The Hemlock Society

Not everyone in the right-to-die movement was happy with the newly renamed Society for the Right to Die and its emphasis on refusing medical treatment, rather than on euthanasia and assisted suicide. One such person was British journalist Derek Humphry.

In 1975 his first wife, Jean, was terminally ill with cancer, and Humphry helped her commit suicide. Encouraged by his second wife, Ann Wickett Humphry, whom he married in 1976, he wrote an account of Jean's assisted suicide, which was published in 1978 as *Jean's Way*. The book was a sensation, both in Britain and the US, and brought Humphry many speaking opportunities, including radio and TV interviews. Soon after its publication, the Humphrys moved to California.

As Humphry began promoting his book and the cause of assisted suicide and euthanasia in the US, he became disillusioned with the right-to-die organizations there, because they focused on passive measures (refusing treatment), not assisted suicide and active euthanasia. Thus in 1980 he formed his own group, the Hemlock Society. It promoted assisted suicide and voluntary euthanasia, primarily for those suffering with terminal illnesses. While pressing for the legalization of what he called "rational suicide," Humphry insisted that he was not encouraging "emotional suicide." Humphry claimed that suicide was only justified if one was enduring unbearable suffering in the face of a terminal illness, or in cases of "grave physical handicap so restricting that the individual cannot, even after due consideration and training, tolerate such a limited existence."[10]

The following year Humphry published *Let Me Die Before I Wake*, a how-to suicide manual aimed at those suffering from terminal illnesses who wanted to end their lives. In the first ten years, it sold 25,000 copies per year. His 1991 book, *Final Exit*, sold over a million copies and was the #4 non-fiction bestseller of the year. Buoyed by the royalties from Humphry's books and the publicity generated by his speaking engagements and radio and TV interviews, the Hemlock Society grew to eighty local chapters and 30,000 members by 1990.[11]

Who joined the Hemlock Society? Over fifty percent of its members were either atheists or agnostics. Less than one-third had some kind of Christian religious identity, and most of those did not attend church regularly. Hemlock Society members who had a religious affiliation were often Unitarians. Indeed, in the early phases of the movement, Humphry's speaking engagements were largely in Unitarian churches.[12]

Explaining Why

In the 1998 book *Freedom to Die: People, Politics, and the Right-to-Die Movement*, Humphry and his co-author, Mary Clement, speculated as to why the right-to-die movement was gaining traction in American society. The authors identified several factors: the stress on individual rights and autonomy arising from the sixties culture, advances in medical technology, the decline in the doctor-patient relationship, the medical profession's poor handling of end-of-life care, and the AIDS epidemic.

Reflecting on the cultural shift of the sixties, they explained one facet of the mentality underlying the push for assisted suicide: "The right-to-die movement is consistent, furthermore, with the baby boomers' increasingly influential creed: 'I want what I want when I want it, especially if it will make me feel better.'"[13]

The authors explained that the primary motivations inducing people to seek assisted suicide were fear of pain, loss of control, the fear of being a burden to others, abandonment and loneliness, the loss of dignity, and the cost of medical care.[14]

Indeed, Humphry thought the cost-cutting effects of assisted sui-cide were a powerful argument for its legalization. He and Clements stated, "Overriding all other considerations, the cost of health care in an aging society demands exploration of a shortening of the dying process to eliminate wasteful procedures and unwanted care."[15] Later in the book they stress the importance of economic motives in driving the right-to-die movement, claiming "one must look at the realities of the increasing cost of health care in an aging society, because in the final analysis, economics, not the quest for broadened individual liber-ties or increased autonomy, will drive assisted suicide to the plateau of acceptable practice."

Immediately after sketching out this economic argument for as-sisted suicide, the authors then ask, "Is there, in fact, a duty to die—a responsibility within the family unit—that should remain voluntary but expected nonetheless?"[16] Note the implications. By implying that people have a duty to die and that under some circumstances assisted suicide should be "expected," Humphry and Clements blur the bound-aries between voluntary and involuntary measures.

This became sadly relevant to Humphry's personal life.

'Til Death Do Us Part

Derek Humphry's second wife, Ann, was diagnosed with breast can-cer in September 1989. Three weeks after her surgery, Humphry left home, supposedly on a business trip, but he left a message on the answering machine telling her that he was not returning. He then removed her from her leadership position in the Hemlock Society and turned all her erstwhile friends and colleagues in the organiza-tion against her.

Feeling (understandably) abandoned by her husband and her friends, Ann reached out to her former ideological enemy, Rita Mark-er, the director of the International Anti-Euthanasia Task Force. Ann informed Marker about her experiences in the right-to-die movement.

In 1991 Ann Humphry committed suicide, even though her cancer was in remission and her illness was not terminal. Thereafter Marker published *Deadly Compassion: The Death of Ann Humphry and the Truth about Euthanasia,* which painted a very unflattering portrait of Derek Humphry. Ann's suicide note was reproduced on the back cover of the book:

> There. You got what you wanted. Ever since I was diagnosed as having cancer, you have done everything conceivable to precipitate my death. I was not alone in recognizing what you were doing. What you did—desertion and abandonment and subsequent harassment of a dying woman—is so unspeakble [sic] there are no words to describe the horror of it. Yet you know. And others know too. You will have to live with this untiol [sic] you die. May you never, ever forget.

The Hemlock Society would go into decline after Derek Humphry resigned from its leadership in 1992. By then they had failed twice in sponsoring ballot initiatives to legalize assisted suicide, one in Washington state in 1991 and one in California in 1992. Humphry, however, continued promoting assisted suicide, forming the Euthanasia Research and Guidance Organization in 1993. When the Hemlock Society changed its name and merged with another organization, becoming Compassion and Choices in 2004, Humphry formed the Final Exit Network.

Jack Kevorkian as Dr. Death

Another player in the US euthanasia movement emerged at about the same time as Derek Humphry. Rather than wait for the legalization of assisted suicide or euthanasia, the flamboyant physician Jack Kevorkian decided to take matters into his own hands by flouting the law.

At a young age Kevorkian, whose parents had survived the Armenian genocide, surmised that God must not exist, because if he did, there would not have been a genocide. Early in his career, nurses nicknamed him Dr. Death because of his fascination with death and dying. Kevorkian proposed doing medical experimentation on willing prisoners during capital punishment, and he performed experiments using blood from corpses for blood transfusions. The paintings he created also reflected morbid themes, such as war or death.[17]

For many years Kevorkian had considered euthanasia and assisted suicide legitimate, and in the late 1980s he decided to act on this conviction. He created a suicide machine, a device that used an intravenous drip and a timer to deliver three successive chemicals into the bloodstream of the person committing suicide. After a 1989 *Newsweek* article mentioned his device, people began contacting him. On June 4, 1990, he used it for the first time to help a fifty-four-year-old woman with Alzheimer's, Janet Adkins, commit suicide. Since there was no law against assisted suicide in Michigan, charges against him were dropped. However, Kevorkian's case prompted the Michigan legislature to pass a temporary law against assisted suicide that was in force from 1991 to 1994. Kevorkian continued assisting in dozens of suicides in the 1990s, and he was prosecuted four times between 1994 and 1997. In the first three trials he was exonerated and the fourth resulted in a hung jury.[18]

In 1998, however, Kevorkian took matters a step further. Thomas Youk, a fifty-two-year-old man with Lou Gehrig's disease, asked for Kevorkian's help in committing suicide. In all of the cases up to that point, Kevorkian had instructed the persons committing suicide to initiate the action that resulted in their death. In this case, however, Kevorkian administered a fatal injection, so this was euthanasia, not assisted suicide.

Further, Kevorkian video-recorded the event and gave it to *60 Minutes*, who broadcast it. This time around Kevorkian represented himself at his trial (unlike his earlier trials) and was convicted of second-degree murder in 1999. According to his biographers, he wanted to lose this case, so he could appeal it to the US Supreme Court.[19] However, to his chagrin, his case was never taken up by the Supreme Court, so he served a prison term until being paroled in 2007 on the condition that he not assist in any more suicides.

Public Relations Disaster

Kevorkian's attitudes and actions alienated many people, including some who were sympathetic with his cause. Derek Humphry, for example, initially encouraged Kevorkian, but quickly realized that

Kevorkian was a public relations disaster for the cause (ironically, considering that he himself had tarnished it). Humphry criticized Kevorkian, claiming he was "too obsessed, too fanatical, in his interest in death and suicide to offer direction for the nation."[20]

Critics also noted that some of the patients Kevorkian assisted in suicide were not in pain, nor were they all terminally ill. In some cases Kevorkian helped them commit suicide within twenty-four hours of actually meeting them for the first time. Though some right-to-die proponents still idolize Kevorkian, it seems likely that he did more harm than good to the movement to legalize assisted suicide.

Bioethics Scholars in the English-Speaking World

Kevorkian was acting in step with theories previously promoted by certain bioethicists. As discussed above, bioethics first emerged in the 1960s and 1970s as a distinct field of study and scholarship. It merged perennial concerns about medical ethics with anxieties about new medical advances and technologies, such as contraception, in vitro fertilization, and dialysis. It also responded to the sixties' desire for greater autonomy and the legalization of abortion. Euthanasia and assisted suicide were major themes in bioethical discourse from the beginning;[21] and in the late twentieth century, some leading bioethicists argued—as Joseph Fletcher did before them—that euthanasia and assisted suicide were morally legitimate and should be legalized.

Peter Singer

Peter Singer, who presently has an endowed chair at Princeton University, is one of the foremost bioethicists in the late twentieth and early twenty-first centuries to favor legalization of assisted suicide and euthanasia. Singer speaks favorably of Darwinism, claiming that it "undermined the foundations of the entire Western way of thinking on the place of our species in the universe," thus demolishing the Judeo-Christian view that human life is special.[22] He embraces Fletcher's personhood theory, arguing that not all human beings have the requisite amount of rationality or consciousness to qualify as full-fledged persons.

In his 1979 book, *Practical Ethics*, Singer based his support for euthanasia on a utilitarian creed that defined morality as that which produces the best consequences and "furthers the interests of those affected."[23] Thus Singer dispensed with ideals such as inherent human rights, including the right to life.

After rejecting the concept of the sanctity of human life, he devoted an entire chapter to euthanasia, wherein he not only argued for voluntary euthanasia, but also for infanticide for infants whose "lives are not worth living," such as those with spina bifida. Singer claimed that people's lives have no value if they are suffering miserably or if they have lost all self-consciousness. Thus, while rejecting involuntary euthanasia (euthanasia against the victim's will), he considered voluntary and nonvoluntary euthanasia permissible (nonvoluntary is when a person does not have the capacity to make a decision, so others decide for that person).[24]

Singer reiterated his support for euthanasia in many subsequent writings. In *Rethinking Life and Death* (1996), for example, he argued that human lives are not equally valuable. Instead, he insisted, we should "recognize that the worth of human life varies." This is because, he asserted, "life without consciousness is of no worth at all." Further, he claimed that instead of trying to dissuade the suicidal, we should adhere to the commandment: "Respect a person's desire to live or die."[25]

Margaret Pabst Battin

A less well-known bioethicist, but one who devoted her career to promoting euthanasia, was Margaret Pabst Battin, a philosophy professor at the University of Utah. In her 2005 book, *Ending Life: Ethics and the Way We Die*, Battin provided two rationales for euthanasia. First, she claimed that we must respect a person's autonomy, which includes the right to choose one's own death. "Just as a person has the right to determine as much as possible the course of his or her own life," she wrote, "a person also has the right to determine as much as possible the course of his or her own dying." Battin argued that people wanting to die can and do make rational choices about death, insisting that not everyone wanting to die is depressed or psychologically unable to make a clear decision.

Second, she argued that the desire to relieve human suffering should motivate us to allow euthanasia.

Ultimately, however, she thought the autonomy argument was much stronger than the argument about alleviating suffering. She considered the strongest argument against assisted suicide and euthanasia the slippery slope argument, though ultimately she did not find it compelling.[26]

Paul Ramsey Pushes Back

Of course, not all bioethicists endorsed euthanasia and assisted suicide. Paul Ramsey was one of the more prominent early bioethicists to reject them, because he believed that human life was inherently valuable. Because of this belief he rejected personhood theory, insisting instead that all human lives have value, regardless of mental or physical abilities.

Ramsey forcefully argued that medical ethics should always militate in favor of saving life, not ending it. Note, however, that he did not oppose withdrawing treatment in futile cases. This, he argued, is not equivalent to euthanasia, because the intent is all-important. Choosing death or intending death, which is the epitome of euthanasia, is morally impermissible, according to Ramsey, but allowing people to die because their bodies are irreversibly dying is completely different. In the latter case, one is not intending death.[27]

The American Medical Profession

Traditionally American physicians have overwhelmingly rejected assisted suicide and euthanasia as incompatible with their profession, which is supposed to save people from death, if possible. Indeed, the American Medical Association (AMA) still opposes assisted suicide and in 2023 specifically rejected a motion that it soften its stance against it. In its *Code of Medical Ethics* the AMA asserts that "permitting physicians to engage in assisted suicide would ultimately cause more harm than good." It further claims that "Physician-assisted suicide is fundamentally incompatible with the physician's role as healer, would be difficult or impossible to control, and would pose serious societal risks." Instead of purposely hastening death, the AMA exhorts physicians to be zealous to provide comfort and pain relief to ease their patients' condition when they are facing imminent death.[28]

Obviously, however, some American physicians today consider assisted suicide legitimate, since they agree to prescribe the deadly doses of drugs in the states that currently allow assisted suicide. A few even publicly encourage assisted suicide and/or euthanasia.

In January 1988, for instance, an anonymous physician published an article in the *Journal of the American Medical Association* (*JAMA*) titled "It's Over, Debbie," endorsing euthanasia. The author wrote that as a young gynecology resident he was called at night to help a young woman who was dying of ovarian cancer. He responded by giving her an overdose of morphine, which killed her. The author portrayed this as a merciful and compassionate deed. Remarkably, however, he admitted that when he perpetrated this deed he was sleepy, and did not even know the patient, and the patient was not requesting assisted suicide or euthanasia.[29] Let that sink in: the patient did not ask to die, but this physician still felt justified in making the decision for her.

This article touched off considerable controversy within the medical community. Later that year an executive editor for *JAMA*, Marcia Angell, published an editorial supporting euthanasia.[30] Five years later Timothy Quill, professor of medicine and psychiatry at the University of Rochester, published a book, *Death and Dignity*, in which he endorsed physician-assisted suicide, though he still opposed all forms of euthanasia. He even admitted to prescribing barbiturates for a patient, knowing that she intended to use them to end her life.[31]

Oregon Embraces Death

In 1994 proponents of physician-assisted suicide scored their first major victory in the United States by barely winning (with 51 percent of the vote) a ballot initiative in Oregon. Legal challenges resulted in a court injunction that delayed implementation of the new law until 1997, the same year Oregon voters again approved—this time with about 60 percent of the vote—the law, known as the Oregon Death with Dignity Act (DWDA).

Initially the Oregon DWDA only allowed assisted suicide for adult residents of Oregon with terminal illnesses. Before prescribing the deadly drugs two physicians had to ascertain that the patient was capable of making his or her own health decisions and was under no compulsion. Further, they had to provide a prognosis of less than six months to live. Patients had to make an oral and written request, and then after a fifteen-day waiting period renew the oral request. Physicians could then write a prescription for a deadly drug, but the patients had to administer it themselves.[32]

Problems with DWDA

One of the more bizarre features of the law is that it stipulates, "Actions taken in accordance with this Act shall not, for any purpose, constitute suicide, assisted suicide, mercy killing or homicide, under the law."[33]

Just about everyone across the ideological spectrum—both proponents and opponents—recognize this as physician-assisted suicide, but Oregon officials studiously reject this term. Not only are they hoping to evade the stigma associated with the term "suicide," but they also recognize there are negative legal ramifications to suicide (such as some life insurance policies not paying out in cases of suicide). Thus, despite the fact that Oregon health officials continue to record the deaths caused by the deadly prescriptions allowed by the DWDA, they do not allow the death certificates of the patients to reflect this reality. They require that the cause of death recorded on the death certificate be the underlying terminal illness, not the ingesting of poison that actually killed them. In sum, the state of Oregon demands that people who fill out death certificates lie about the actual cause of death.

Critics of the Oregon DWDA point out that once the deadly prescription is granted to a patient, there is no further oversight. In theory the drug is supposed to be self-administered, but there is no way to know if this actually happens. If a patient takes the drug home and is later coerced or even given the drug unaware, no one would ever know.

Another problem with this law is that it assumes that physicians have precise knowledge about the future of an ill patient. To be sure, many physicians do have enough experience with patients with terminal illnesses to give an educated guess about the time they have remaining before death. However, in Oregon quite a few recipients of the deadly drugs have had them longer than six months, meaning physicians were either mistaken or else purposely gave a false prognosis to allow the patient to qualify for assisted suicide. When Alice Bozeman's physician told her in 2009 that her terminal lung illness would result in her death within six months, and then hinted that she might want to apply for assisted suicide, she refused. She lived almost twelve more years, passing away in 2021. During these years of her life she was able to greet some new grandchildren and also see some of her grandchildren get married.

Consider, as well, the controversial case of a physician in Colorado in 2022 who prescribed assisted suicide drugs to three patients suffering from the eating disorder anorexia nervosa. One of these patients, a thirty-six-year-old woman, ingested the poison and ended her life. She probably could have survived for decades, if she had only begun eating food, instead of a deadly dose of drugs.[34]

Expanding DWDA

As in other jurisdictions that have legalized assisted suicide and/or euthanasia, Oregon's program began rather modestly. In 1998 only sixteen people died from assisted suicide, which was a mere 0.06 percent of the total deaths in that state. However, in the ensuing years the numbers have steadily climbed. The DWDA report of 2021 shows that 259 patients in 2020 ingested a deadly dose of medication, which is about 0.7 percent of Oregon's total deaths.[35]

In the years since 1997, proponents of assisted suicide have lobbied to expand access to assisted suicide in Oregon by eliminating legal restrictions. Since 2020 Oregon has waived the fifteen-day waiting period in cases where physicians suspect the patient will not live longer than fifteen days. In 2021 this resulted in 21 percent of the DWDA recipients having the fifteen-day rule waived. Further, in 2022 Oregon ended its residency requirement, so now anyone with a terminal illness can travel to Oregon to receive a deadly prescription. Officials in Oregon have also been rather broad in their interpretation of what constitutes a terminal illness. They have admitted that people would qualify for assisted suicide if they quit taking insulin or some other life-sustaining medication.

Pain Isn't the Primary Reason

One of the ways that assisted suicide proponents have convinced the public to accept assisted suicide is by stressing the pain and agony that many suffer in the final throes of their illnesses. However, the Oregon DWDA says nothing at all about the patient having to be in pain or suffering to qualify for assisted suicide.

Interestingly, health officials in Oregon survey patients about why they are seeking assisted suicide. In the first ten years of assisted suicide in Oregon, less than one-third of all patients reported that pain or the fear of pain played a role in their decision to seek assisted suicide.[36] In the 2020 survey, again, less than a third reported that pain played a role, though over half indicated that they were concerned about being a burden to their family and others.[37] In 2021, as in other years, the three most frequently reported reasons for seeking assisted suicide were: loss of autonomy (93 percent), decreasing ability to participate in enjoyable activities (92 percent), and loss of dignity (68 percent). (The percentages are more than 100 percent because respondents could choose more than one reason—which makes it all the more remarkable that less than one-third mentioned pain as a factor in their decision).[38]

States' Rights

While Oregon was pursuing legalization of assisted suicide in the mid-1990s, advocates of assisted suicide were challenging other states' laws prohibiting assisted suicide.

In 1994 assisted suicide proponents brought two cases, *Washington v. Glucksberg* and *Vacco v. Quill* (the latter in New York), arguing that state laws banning assisted suicide violated the US Constitution.

In *Glucksberg* both the district and appellate court ruled against the state of Washington's ban on assisted suicide. In *Quill* the district court ruled in favor of the state of New York's ban, but the appellate court reversed this. In 1997 the Supreme Court took up both these cases and unanimously overturned the appellate courts' decisions, affirming that laws prohibiting assisted suicide are not unconstitutional.[39] This decision left it up to the states to determine the legality of assisted suicide.

Since 1997 assisted suicide proponents have focused on state legislatures, introducing legislation in many states to try to legalize it. Most of these efforts have failed, especially before 2015. However, in the past decade their efforts have resulted in the legalization of assisted suicide in several states. By 2023 ten jurisdictions in the US passed laws legalizing assisted suicide: California, Colorado, District of Columbia, Hawaii, Maine, New Jersey, New Mexico, Oregon, Vermont, and Washington. In addition, a court in Montana in 2009 ruled that no Montana law forbade assisted suicide, so assisted suicide is legal there as well, though it is not regulated by any law.

Most of the states allowing physician-assisted suicide modeled their laws on the Oregon DWDA. Washington, the second state to legalize assisted suicide, even named its law the Death with Dignity Act. In a 2008 referendum there, 58 percent of the voters approved of physician-assisted suicide.[40] Assisted suicide proponents gained another major victory in 2016 when the legislature of the most populous state in the US, California, passed (and the governor signed) the End of Life Option Act, which legalized physician-assisted suicide.

Physician-assisted suicide is still illegal in forty states, and euthanasia is still illegal everywhere in the US.

Continuing Opposition to Assisted Suicide in the US

Despite significant gains by assisted suicide advocates, bills to legalize assisted suicide have been defeated repeatedly in many states. The clash between those opposing and those favoring legalization of physician-assisted suicide continues in earnest in the US.

Religious Groups

In the late twentieth and early twenty-first centuries, the staunchest opposition to assisted suicide in the US has come from religious organizations and individuals. The Catholic Church continues to oppose assisted suicide and euthanasia. Indeed, in the late twentieth century Pope John Paul II popularized use of the term "culture of death" to describe the present worldwide movement toward legalizing abortion, euthanasia, and assisted suicide. He campaigned vigorously against these deadly practices, and he insisted that assisting someone to commit suicide is equivalent to murder.[41]

Conservative Protestant denominations and churches also reject assisted suicide and euthanasia. In 1996 the Southern Baptist Convention, for instance, passed a resolution opposing assisted suicide and imploring governments to prosecute physicians who engage in it.[42]

Disability Organizations

Religious groups are not the only ones wary of assisted suicide and euthanasia. Many disability organizations are likewise concerned about the increasing acceptance of assisted suicide. A major disability rights organization, the Disability Rights Education and Defense Fund, founded in 1979, has published a guide on their website, "Why Assisted Suicide Must Not Be Legalized." They suspect that the many prejudices against people with disabilities will mean that they will be targets of assisted suicide.

This group points out that people dying through assisted suicide indicate that their reasons for killing themselves are primarily not particular crises (pain or terminal illness, for instance), but rather a desire not to live with disabilities. Because assisted suicide is cheaper than good health care, this incentivizes insurance companies and health providers to offer assisted suicide, rather than other more expensive alternatives that could extend a patient's life. Further, they also point out that safeguards attached to the assisted suicide laws in the US, which allegedly protect people, are rather flimsy and invite abuse.[43]

In 1996 some people with disabilities founded an organization, Not Dead Yet, whose primary mission is to oppose the legalization of assisted suicide and euthanasia.

Judicial Scholars

Some judicial scholars have also expressed opposition to the legalization of assisted suicide and euthanasia. In 2006 Neil Gorsuch, who later became a US Supreme Court Justice, published *The Future of Assisted Suicide and Euthanasia* with Princeton University Press. In that book he set forth a secular argument against assisted suicide and euthanasia. He laid out his position thus: "It is an argument premised on the idea that all human beings are intrinsically valuable and the intentional taking of human life by private persons is always wrong."[44]

In his book Gorsuch argues that human life is a basic good, not something whose value fluctuates depending on various characteristics it exhibits (as Fletcher, Singer, and other personhood theorists maintain). He also explains that his position allows for ending medical treatment, even if it results in death, as long as the intent is not suicidal.

Canada Lunges Forward

Canada's move toward legalizing assisted suicide and euthanasia began in 2015, when the Canadian Supreme Court argued that the ban against assisted dying was unconstitutional.

The following year the Canadian parliament legalized both assisted suicide and euthanasia, calling them collectively Medical Assistance in Dying (MAiD). Under this new law adult Canadian patients who have a "grievous and irremediable medical condition" can request assisted suicide or euthanasia. The law clarifies that the qualifying medical condition must be "in an advanced state of irreversible decline wherein the patient is experiencing intolerable suffering and whose natural death has become reasonably foreseeable." Two physicians or nurse practitioners must confirm that the patient is eligible, and after the patient's request there must be a ten-day waiting period, unless the patient has less than ten days to live.[45]

In 2017, the first full year that MAiD was in effect, 2,838 patients ended their lives with the help of a physician or nurse. The numbers dying under MAiD have increased dramatically every year, reaching 10,064 in 2021, which constituted about 3.3 percent of the total deaths in Canada. This brought the total number of Canadians dying under MAiD since its legalization to 31,644.

The Canadian government has also expanded eligibility for MAiD. In 2019 a court in Quebec ruled that the requirement that a patient's death must be reasonably foreseeable was illegal. Prime Minister Justin Trudeau and his government, who are strong proponents of MAiD, decided not to appeal the court case, but to bring Canadian law into line with the court ruling. Thus, in 2021 Canada dropped the requirement that a person must be terminally ill, and 219 people who died under MAiD in 2021 were not terminally ill. The 2021 MAiD law also opened the door for MAiD for patients who are suffering only from a mental illness, though it delayed that eligibility until March 17, 2023. Because of widespread concern and opposition to allowing MAiD for people with mental illnesses, the Canadian government announced that it would delay implementation for another year, pushing it back to March 2024.[46] Then, in February 2024, the Canadian government voted to again delay implementation, this time to March 2027.[47]

Death as a Cure for Poverty

Canadian government surveys of people requesting MAiD show that the "intolerable suffering" that the law mentions as an eligibility requirement is usually not physical pain. Rather, the most commonly cited reason for MAiD was "loss of ability to engage in meaningful activities" (86 percent in the 2021 survey), followed closely by "loss of ability to perform activities of daily life" (83 percent).[48]

In a few high-profile cases in Canada, people with various illnesses have requested MAiD not because of the illnesses they have (which only serve as the excuse to gain them eligibility), but because they lack housing or social services. In 2022 a fifty-four-year-old man, Amir Farsoud, who suffers considerable pain from a back injury, applied for

MAiD. His painful condition would likely qualify him for MAiD. However, he was not applying because of his physical pain, but because the home he was renting was up for sale and his income was too meager to find other housing. As he explained, "I don't want to die but I don't want to be homeless more than I don't want to die."[49]

In 2023 a homeless man in Ontario, 37-year-old Tyler Dunlop, also applied for MAiD because his homelessness brought him to despair for his future and caused him to suffer social isolation. Dunlop is not physically ill in any way, but he explained, "I looked at my future, and I said, 'What am I going to be in the next 10 years?' Same thing: wandering around homeless."[50] Thus, some desperate Canadians view MAiD as a way to escape poverty, homelessness, or other problems spawned by inadequate income or social services.

Creeping Forward

Until the late twentieth century euthanasia and assisted suicide were illegal everywhere in the US and Canada. Oregon broke that taboo in 1997 by legalizing assisted suicide—but not euthanasia—for those with terminal illnesses. Since then, ten states plus Washington DC have legalized assisted suicide.

Assisted suicide is still illegal in forty states of the US, but assisted suicide proponents are actively lobbying in many states to overturn the prohibitions on assisted suicide. Polling in the US suggests that many Americans support assisted suicide for those with terminal illnesses, so unless public opinion shifts, it seems likely that more states will eventually legalize assisted suicide.

Canada has gone even further by legalizing euthanasia and assisted suicide in 2016. Further, since 2021 Canadians don't even have to have a terminal illness to qualify for euthanasia. They only have to get two physicians to certify that they are suffering intolerably.

Based on the track record of the past few generations, the cultural movement towards death would seem to be a slippery slope. In the chapters to follow I will seek to show that it is, but not quite an inevitable one. Indeed, the trend can be reversed.

8. EUTHANASIA'S END GAME

IN THE SPRING OF 2023 A YOUNG WOMAN, KATHRIN MENTLER, sought help at the Vancouver General Hospital's Access and Assessment Center. She was suffering from depression and anxiety, and in the past she had repeatedly attempted suicide.

"That day," she explained, "my goal was to keep myself safe. I was thinking of maybe trying to get myself admitted to hospital because I was in crisis." The counselor who met with her told her that the mental health system was overwhelmed, so she would not be able to get help immediately. Then the counselor shocked her by asking if she would like to apply for euthanasia based on her mental suffering.

Mentler, who was hoping for help resisting suicidal thoughts that day, described how the counselor's advice affected her: "That made me feel like my life was worthless or a problem that could be solved if I chose MAiD [i.e., euthanasia]."

The story is distressing on multiple levels. It shows how the euthanasia option can and does become a means of sidestepping the hard work of providing care to the suffering. And since the story involves euthanasia being offered to someone merely because the person was in emotional crisis, it illustrates how the circle of people deemed eligible for euthanasia or assisted suicide keeps widening, confirming the validity of worries that, once a line has been crossed, the culture of death will tend to spread. Indeed, the subtitle of the article reporting on Mentler's case stated, "Experts say Kathrin Mentler's experience is indicative of a slippery slope when it comes to health care for mentally ill and disabled patients."[1]

Assessing the Slippery Slope Argument

The slippery slope argument is often used by opponents of assisted suicide and euthanasia to warn of the dangers of legalization. The legal scholar John Keown is one of the more articulate opponents of assisted suicide, arguing that legalizing voluntary physician-assisted suicide in strictly prescribed cases is likely to open a Pandora's box, giving rise to a progressive widening of cases deemed legally acceptable for assisted suicide, as well as increasing acceptance of both voluntary and involuntary euthanasia.[2]

Further, many opponents of assisted suicide point to the history of assisted suicide and euthanasia as confirmation of the slippery slope. The Nazi program to kill people with disabilities is the most sobering specter. However, even if one dismisses this episode as an aberration—as most proponents of assisted suicide do—more recent developments in the Netherlands, Belgium, Canada, and the US also arouse concerns about a slippery slope. The psychiatrist Mark Komrad makes just such a case, arguing that the recent trajectory of assisted suicide in these countries has already demonstrated the reality of the slippery slope.[3]

Some advocates of assisted suicide, such as the philosopher Margaret Pabst Battin, consider the slippery slope argument to carry some force.[4] However, others dismiss the slippery slope argument, claiming it lacks logical rigor. They argue, for instance, that legalizing voluntary assisted suicide for patients with terminal illnesses (often Oregon's law is taken as a model here) does not lead to a slippery slope toward involuntary euthanasia, or assisted suicide for psychological problems, or other abuses. They assure the public that assisted suicide and euthanasia can be kept safely within reasonable limits.

Some versions of the slippery slope argument against assisted suicide are indeed overstated. Supporting voluntary assisted suicide does not logically entail acceptance of involuntary euthanasia, as some suggest. Nor does accepting assisted suicide for people with terminal illnesses logically entail acceptance of assisted suicide for others without terminal illnesses.

Nonetheless, the slippery slope criticism still has merit. I will provide three arguments to demonstrate its validity, while also examining historical developments that corroborate this position.

Before I do so, let me take issue with one other aspect of a common version of the slippery slope argument against assisted suicide, namely the view that the first step on the path toward assisted suicide is not itself immoral, but taking that step will inevitably lead to further steps that are morally problematic. However, I consider the first step toward assisted suicide and/or euthanasia morally wrong. It is not just that opening the door to assisted suicide leads to abuses and immoral behavior. No, I am firmly convinced that any kind of assisted suicide is immoral in and of itself. Thus the slippery slope argument as it is commonly formulated concedes too much to proponents of assisted suicide and euthanasia.

On to my three arguments.

Point One: Denial of Human Equality

First and most importantly, in order to accept physician-assisted suicide as legitimate, one must abandon the view that all human lives are valuable, and this erases a crucial distinction that protects human life.

A society that legalizes assisted suicide is denying human equality, because the legislators have to decide which humans can be killed via assisted suicide and which cannot. De facto, they are saying that some lives are valuable, but others are not. Governments that are spending large sums of money to prevent suicides of people deemed valuable would simultaneously be giving their approval for other people to commit suicide. Thus legislators are clearly making a value judgment: some people's lives are so valuable that we should do everything possible to dissuade them from committing suicide; however, others' lives are worth so little that we will help them kill themselves.

This abandonment of human equality and the concomitant rejection of the notion that all human lives have value sets us on the slippery slope, because the categories of people deemed valuable and those considered less valuable or even without any value are subject to the whim of those drawing up the legislation. Surely if history has taught us anything, it has taught us that "experts" and "authorities" are fallible and as prone to corruption as anyone else.

Can "Person" Adequately Replace "Human"?

Once we no longer use the category of "human" as decisive in determining the value of a human being, there is no clearly defined category to replace it. To be sure, bioethicists who embrace "personhood theory"—Joseph Fletcher, Peter Singer, and many others—have proposed criteria to define a "person" apart from membership in the human family. However, they do not agree among themselves on the criteria, and the criteria they propose are very ill-defined.

For instance, when I debated Peter Singer on a radio program about the question, "Is human life intrinsically valuable?" I mentioned that Fletcher had proposed various traits to define personhood that differed in some ways from those advanced by Singer. When I then asked Singer why he chose the particular traits he did, I was astonished that he didn't have a ready answer to justify his definition. Instead, he suggested that the traits are open to discussion.[5] This is a remarkable admission, because his whole view of who qualifies as a person—and thus possesses a right to life—hinges on these particular traits. And yet those traits are negotiable?

Singer has been notoriously difficult to pin down on when a human being has the requisite rationality and self-consciousness to be considered a person. He claims that newborn infants, even if perfectly healthy, should not be considered persons and thus have no right to life, but he refuses to designate a particular age when a human being becomes a person. (Indeed, the logic of his position would suggest that different human beings become "persons" at different ages, depending on their mental development.)[6]

So definitions of personhood are ultimately arbitrary and ill-defined. This in and of itself shows that personhood theory ushers us down the slippery slope, because it provides a fig-leaf rationale for arbitrary and involuntary euthanasia. Those judged to be "non-persons" (for whatever reason) can be killed, against their will or without their permission, by those judged to be "persons."

Note, further, that under personhood theory some people aren't safe from euthanasia proponents. "Persons" (people having a certain level of consciousness) may be worthy of life, and can only be killed if they so wish, on the grounds of autonomy. But those judged to be "non-persons" (people lacking a certain level of consciousness) are unworthy of life and can be killed without their permission.

So if "personhood" is a poor substitute for "being a human being" as the relevant category for securely adjudicating who does and doesn't deserve protection from being killed, then what category would be adequate?

Suffering and Terminal Illness

Perhaps we can gain clarity from legislation. What criteria do assisted-suicide proponents hope to enshrine in law to prevent abuse and avoid a slippery slope?

Presently most US states that have legalized assisted suicide only allow it for those with terminal illnesses and deemed by physicians to be in the last six months of their life. Other jurisdictions with assisted suicide, such as the Netherlands and Belgium, include far more people in their scope. The 2002 Dutch law legalizing voluntary active euthanasia allowed it for any patient whose "suffering was lasting and unbearable."

But why? If assisted suicide is permissible, there does not seem to be any rigorous philosophical reason to restrict it to those with terminal illnesses, to those with six months to live, or even to those who are suffering. These criteria are arbitrary. Why six months and not twelve months or two years? Why not include people with non-terminal, incurable illnesses? Who can say across the board what suffering is "lasting" or "unbearable"? There is no clear rationale for these boundaries, and this opens the door to widening the categories.

And indeed, in practice these boundaries have proven to be elastic.[7] Some patients in Oregon who have requested medication to terminate their life have had their prescriptions for assisted suicide much longer than six months, so obviously their physicians erred in their calculations (and we cannot know whether this was accidental or purposeful). Surprisingly, even the notion of what constitutes a "terminal illness" is flexible. Oregon officials have admitted that dialysis patients who decide to forgo dialysis could be considered terminal patients with less than six months to live, and would thus qualify for assisted suicide, even though they could live for decades if they stayed on dialysis. I wonder how many Oregon voters and legislators considered a dialysis patient a terminally ill patient when the legislation was initially passed.

As for suffering, it is a notoriously difficult concept to define, since it is completely subjective. Consider physical pain: it is impossible to know exactly how much someone else is hurting, even with the monitoring of blood pressure and pulse, which can be elevated by a variety of factors. Moreover, pain is to some degree a state of mind. Pain clinics often teach patients to "reframe" pain, which reduces anxiety, which often leads to a reduction in the experienced pain itself. None of this is meant to imply that pain is not real; of course it is, and compassion dictates that those suffering from it be offered a full spectrum of palliative therapies (ideally including, I would add, supportive companionship, which has been shown to significantly reduce perceptions of pain). But my point here is that "pain" is well-nigh impossible to define or measure objectively.

Further, many people assume that "suffering" refers to physical pain. But as we have seen, physical pain ranks relatively low on the reasons people give for wishing to die, and Canada, Switzerland, the Netherlands, and Belgium, as well as the state of Oregon, include psychological afflictions under the umbrella term "suffering." Psychological suffering is even more subjective than physical pain (which can at least be connected to objectively verifiable ailments such as cancer), and even less amenable to time-of-duration assessments. Some people with mental illnesses, for instance, see an easing of symptoms as they age. Some people experience seasonal swings in their psychological distress—so, yes, they may have extreme suffering all their lives, but only periodically. Such fluctuations and unpredictability make psychological distress a highly elastic category.

Basing qualification standards on such categories surely contributes to the slipperiness of the slope. Consider a study published in 2023 examining 927 cases that the Dutch euthanasia review board posted to its website. The investigators discovered that thirty-nine of those cases involved patients with intellectual disabilities and/or autism. One case file stated that the patient "had never been able to keep up with society, he had become insecure, with recurring depression. Due to his intellectual disability, he felt a great pressure of the world on him which he could not handle. His autistic traits made it increasingly difficult for him to cope with changes around him." In this study the most common cause of "unbearable suffering" was "social isolation/loneliness," which 77 percent indicated as a contributing factor. Other major reasons for these people with mental disabilities seeking euthanasia were dependence, poor quality of life, and loss of hope.[8]

The Australian bioethicist Gregory Pike, in an essay arguing that support for voluntary euthanasia leads down a slippery slope toward killing those with mental problems, highlights case studies of psychiatric euthanasia in the Netherlands from 2012 to 2015. In one, as noted earlier, the "patient indicated that she had had a life without love and therefore had no right to exist." Another patient "was an utterly lonely man whose life had been a failure." Another patient was a woman who "suffered from the meaninglessness of her existence, the lack of a prospect of a future and the continuous feeling of finding herself in a black hole... she experienced deep despair and loneliness." (All these quotations are from the Dutch regional euthanasia review committees that oversee euthanasia.) The Dutch physicians administering euthanasia agreed with their patients that these problems constituted "unbearable suffering," thus qualifying for euthanasia.[9]

It is surely a slippery slope that begins with killing someone in extreme, terminal physical pain and ends with killing someone for being lonely. But, again, this shouldn't surprise us. "Unbearable and lasting suffering" is impossible to clearly demarcate. And because of the subjective and arbitrary nature of this line, it's about as much use as no line at all. Thus, in 2001 the Dutch Health Minister Els Borst stated that elderly people who are tired of life should be offered assisted suicide,[10] and some people are already availing themselves of this option. In a highly publicized act in 2018 the 104-year-old Australian scientist, David Goodall, flew to Switzerland to commit suicide, even though he had neither terminal illness nor chronic pain.[11]

Assisted Suicide or Execution?

A recent case in Belgium vividly illustrates the elasticity of the supposed safeguards for assisted suicide. In 2007 Genevieve Lhermitte murdered her five children and then attempted suicide. She survived, was convicted of murder, and was sentenced to life in prison. In 2019 she was transferred to a psychiatric facility.

In 2023 Belgian physicians euthanized her at her request, because she was suffering in her circumstances.[12] But as one critic noted:

> You wonder where the logic of personal autonomy will end. Prisoners must be amongst the most vulnerable people of all possible candidates for euthanasia. Their surroundings seem purpose-made to inspire despair and promote groupthink. Their custodians benefit from their deaths by cutting costs. They are already being punished by restricting the exercise of their autonomy. It seems perverse to allow them to choose death when they cannot even choose their favourite TV program.[13]

What is especially bizarre about this is that Belgium, along with many other European countries, has banned executions, because Belgians consider them barbaric and outmoded. However, now, under the guise of euthanasia, they are allowing it for prisoners who no longer want to live in prison.

This is not the only case of prisoners being euthanized, either. Canada has euthanized nine prisoners in its first seven years of legalized euthanasia. Truly it appears that "the death penalty is creeping back through a rear door."[14]

Thus we can clearly see the arbitrariness and elasticity of the categories that supposedly serve as safeguards. Once the firm principle that "all human lives are sacred" is discarded, down the slippery slope we go. As John Keown eloquently argued, all the limitations on assisted suicide imposed by law ultimately give way, "because the case for euthanasia with those limitations is also, logically, a case for euthanasia without them."[15]

Point Two: Pressure to End One's Life

Now I turn to my second argument confirming the slippery slope argument: legalization of assisted suicide sends a powerful message that some people's lives are no longer deemed valuable enough to protect. In doing so it puts pressure on such people to end their lives, either because they view themselves as a burden to relatives and friends, or because they regret the financial outlay for their healthcare. Because humans are subject to social pressure, the boundary between voluntary and involuntary suicide and euthanasia is porous.

Sometimes the pressure to end one's life may be direct, as other people encourage the patient to commit suicide. For example, in 2022 a Canadian man named Roger Foley reported that officials at the hospital where he had run up huge bills wanted him to accept euthanasia. He stated that they "asked if I want an assisted death. I don't. I was told that I would be charged $1,800 per day [for hospital care]. I have $2 million worth of bills. Nurses here told me that I should end my life. That shocked me."[16]

Pressure to accept assisted suicide and euthanasia is by no means uncommon in countries where it is legal, even if the pressure may sometimes be more subtle than in Foley's case. As we have seen in the historical chapters above, all sorts of people—from physicians to case workers to family members—have suggested to people with illnesses or disabilities that they could end their lives. This should come as no surprise—indeed, it was foreseen in the early days of pro-death legislation. When the British House of Lords debated voluntary euthanasia in 1969, Lady Summerskill reminded the peers that "undoubtedly there will be someone to remind the invalid of his newly acquired powers over his own disposal."[17] She was not wrong. In 2024 Matthew Parris, one of the UK's leading commentators and a former member of Parliament, commented, "As to adding pressure upon the terminally ill to lift the burden they're placing on others… well, let me bite the bullet. In time, I think that the spread and acceptance of assisted dying may indeed do that. And let me bite deeper into the bullet. I think this would be a good thing."[18]

Further, those exerting pressure may even take matters into their own hands. There is ample room for this, for example, in the way that assisted suicide is practiced in the US. The law in most US states (modeled on the Oregon law) stipulates that a patient must voluntarily request the lethal medication. In theory, the patient is then supposed to take the fatal dose at the time and place of his or her choosing. What could be more voluntary? However, though the request for the prescription is—if done according to law—voluntary, once the prescription is filled, there is no way of knowing if its ingestion is voluntary or not. No supervision is required, so we cannot know if the patients voluntarily followed through, or if someone else urged, deceived, or even forced them to end their lives.

Moreover, even when no one is overtly encouraging struggling people to commit suicide, they may conclude that their lives are burdensome. They may see close family members sacrificing greatly, both in time and money, to care for them. In such cases they may conclude that, out of compassion for others, they should terminate their lives. Indeed, when recipients of euthanasia or assisted suicide in Canada and Oregon have been surveyed about why they wanted to die, many have indicated that one of the reasons they want to end their lives is that they feel like a burden on their family or on others.

Statistics suggest that people who have a viable network of family and friends are less likely to ask for assisted suicide. Showing love and concern for an individual may keep them from even considering this option. An alternative to the loneliness of radical individualism are the healthy ties of family, a faith community, or even a close-knit neighborhood, ties animated by the ethos, "We take care of each other." This is the sort of culture that gives and receives, with each person assuming that sometimes he or she will be the giver, and sometimes the recipient. Parents care for small children; children grow up and care for elderly parents. This is a healthy cycle of life, and in such a community of mutual support, both givers and recipients benefit. Givers learn to think of others, even to sacrifice for others; recipients learn to accept their own frailties and to graciously accept help. Everyone gives and receives mercy and grace. Everyone learns patience and passes beyond it to love. Everyone develops deeper, stronger, richer characters than they would otherwise have had.

All this is possible, and all this goes against the prevailing notion of the individual who does what he pleases, standing alone until, alone, he falls. Such a culture says, "I don't have time for you." It says that people who inconvenience us or make us uncomfortable should consider removing themselves from the planet. It says that if you're hurting, I won't sit with you and comfort you and walk alongside you as you learn the hard but worthwhile lessons taught by struggle and suffering and hardship. I won't go through the darkness with you; you're on your own.

Legalization of assisted suicide, while touted by proponents as merely allowing people to do what they already want to do, fosters just such a culture of isolation and rejection. It also raises the possibility of suicide to people who otherwise may not have considered it. It is well known that suicide in general is contagious, with media coverage of suicides often spawning a wave of copycat suicides. Because of this, suicide prevention advocates have issued media guidelines for journalists writing about suicides, lest media coverage contribute to further suicides. What makes us think that assisted suicide is not also contagious?

In this way, then, the floodgates are open, and the slippery slope hurries more and more people towards death.

Point Three: Altering the Role of Physicians in Health Care

My third and final argument confirming the slippery slope argument is that physician-assisted suicide blurs the boundary between healing and killing in the minds of physicians.

In order to aid in assisted suicide, physicians have to dispense with the Hippocratic Oath and its prohibition against helping patients kill themselves. Until very recently Western medical ethics has uniformly rejected physician involvement in assisted suicide, because the medical profession focused on helping restore health and bringing life, not hastening death. This protected both patients and physicians.

However, when physicians participate in assisted suicide, they have to make determinations about the quality of their patients' lives. Is their suffering unbearable? Is their illness—whether physical or mental—incurable? Essentially, in order for physicians to participate in assisted suicide, they have to make determinations about which patients' lives have value and which do not.

Making judgments about the quality of other peoples' lives is not only difficult, but pernicious. Consider the previously mentioned example of Virginia Woolf. Under contemporary laws in some countries, Woolf would be able to request assisted suicide for herself on the grounds of unbearable mental suffering. But if you recall, Woolf looked at a group of mentally impaired people and said *they* should be put to death.[19] Those people would not be capable of consenting to euthanasia. And in fact many people who have no ability to consent to a voluntary death often would be judged as having less quality of life than those granted euthanasia. Once physicians accept that some individuals' lives are worth so little that they may be put to death, it is only a small step to begin putting to death involuntarily those deemed of lesser value.[20]

This is not a hypothetical supposition. In the Netherlands, where voluntary euthanasia is accepted practice, surveys of physicians have shown that some of them do indeed hasten patients' deaths without authorization from the patients.[21] And making a murky situation even murkier, euthanized patients are in some places allowed to be organ donors. (As you might expect, patients euthanized for psychological suffering leave behind healthier organs than those euthanized for disease.)[22] Thus, the same hospital might have patients waiting for organs, and vulnerable psychiatric patients who could be persuaded to die and donate organs.

Another problem for physicians is that once society deems assisted suicide a fundamental right—and many assisted suicide proponents argue that it is—then physicians' involvement will likely become expected or maybe even required. Most jurisdictions that allow assisted suicide currently do not require physicians to participate. However, the pressure on physicians is building, and in Ontario, Canada, courts have trampled on physicians' conscience rights by demanding that they either participate themselves or refer patients to physicians who will comply with their wish to kill themselves.[23]

Further, as has been mentioned, in some US jurisdictions that allow assisted suicide, physicians who choose to participate are being required by law to engage in unethical behavior, namely, falsifying the death certificate. In Oregon and in other states following its lead, physicians are required by law not to list the actual cause of death—that is, the poison they prescribed—but to ascribe the death to the terminal illness the patient had. Thus, physicians are being asked to lie to cover up the unpleasant reality of suicide.

So we see here a slippery slope in which the physician moves from healer to killer, coercer, and liar.

End Game

The slippery slope argument is in fact a powerful argument against assisted suicide and euthanasia. The logical boundaries that many assisted suicide proponents try to erect to keep us from careening down the slippery slope are either arbitrary or elastic. Thus, many of these "safeguards," when they come to be seen as hindrances, are then acknowledged to be logically arbitrary barriers and swept aside by advocates of assisted suicide and euthanasia. The result is more and more deaths—not all of them voluntary—for more and more "reasons."

A host of other ills may cascade from the legalization of euthanasia and assisted suicide: an erosion of trust among family and community; a growing sense of isolation and rejection; and a weakening of the mutual give-and-take fabric of a healthy society. We also see the integrity of the physician crumbling as doctors are asked to become judges, executioners, and deceivers.

The only way to avoid the slippery slope leading to such a culture of death is to promote the dignity and value of every human life and to offer love and compassion to those who are suffering, rather than encourage them to kill themselves.

9. Doing As I Please

Dr. Kenneth Stevens, a physician in Oregon, once had a patient named Jeanette Hall who suffered from rectal cancer. He recommended life-saving chemotherapy treatment, but Hall refused. She could not bear the thought of losing her hair from the chemotherapy. Instead she requested assisted suicide, legal in that state.

Instead of jotting out a prescription for the poisonous drug used in assisted suicide, Stevens compassionately asked Hall about her family. Based on their conversation, Hall realized that she did have a reason to live. She reconsidered her desire for assisted suicide and accepted the treatment, which—as expected—caused her to lose her hair. But she coped with that, and five years later she thanked Dr. Stevens, telling him, "You saved my life. If I had gone to a doctor that believed in assisted suicide I would not be here. I'd be dead."[1]

The Autonomy Argument

This vignette illustrates some of the problems with the autonomy argument, which euthanasia advocates consider one of the strongest arguments in favor of euthanasia and assisted suicide. Margaret Pabst Battin, a philosopher who has devoted her career to promoting assisted suicide, argues that the autonomy argument is the strongest argument in the philosophical arsenal of those advocating for assisted suicide. She summarizes the argument in this way: "Just as a person has the right to determine as much as possible the course of his or her own life, a person also has the right to determine as much as possible the course of his or her own dying."[2]

The term "autonomy" comes from two root words that mean "self-law," so the term literally means being a law unto oneself. It denotes the freedom to make choices about one's own life. This sounds very appealing, as we all crave freedom. No one likes being told what to do. But legalizing assisted suicide and euthanasia does not in fact make us masters of our own fates. Assisted suicide and euthanasia laws in fact restrict our autonomy in important ways and, moreover, ignore serious questions regarding the extent to which one can make an autonomous, authentic decision regarding one's own death. In reality we can never be wholly autonomous, nor should we want to be; no man is an island.

First, consider this: If Dr. Stevens had complied with Hall's initial request to help her end her life, proponents of assisted suicide would have congratulated him for respecting her autonomy. And she would be dead. This is the irony at the heart of the autonomy argument for assisted suicide. How does being dead contribute to personal autonomy? Rather, it robs us of autonomy, because it ends our ability to make free choices (unless one believes that one's autonomy continues on into an afterlife, but this raises other problems for assisted suicide).

There is considerable discussion about the concept of autonomy: whether it is an "instrumental" value (that is, useful as a tool leading to other valuable ends such as happiness) or is unconditionally valuable (valuable in and of itself, whether or not it leads to other valuable ends); whether achieving certain valuable ends can only be accomplished by abridging autonomy; whether autonomy is of primary importance; and so forth. Such conversations serve to underline the point that whatever else might be said about it, autonomy is the purview of living human beings.[3]

Ole Hartling, former chair of Denmark's Council of Ethics (and who cared for first one wife, and then another, through their lengthy terminal illnesses), put it this way:

> An inherent problem of autonomy in connection with assisted dying is that a person who uses his or her presumed right to self-determination to choose death definitively precludes him or herself from deciding or choosing anything. Where death is concerned,

your right to self-determination can only be exerted by disposing of it for good. By your autonomy, in other words, you opt to no longer have autonomy.[4]

Dr. Stevens actually contributed to the greater flourishing of Jeanette Hall's autonomy by convincing her not to commit suicide. By choosing life she could continue making choices.

Restricting Autonomy

Those who think everyone should be able to choose his or her own death should, logically speaking, oppose any restrictions in assisted suicide and euthanasia laws regarding who, when, or why. And yet almost everyone agrees that such laws should contain restrictions— both legal safeguards to protect people from themselves, and overseers (generally physicians) to enforce and implement the laws. This flies in the face of patient autonomy.

First there are the legal requirements—terminal illness, unbearable suffering, and so forth. These limit the exercising of autonomy. Then, if a patient meets the criteria and proceeds through the process, it is the doctor—and not the patient—who wields authority over the patient's life and death.

As psychiatrists Ronald Pies and Cynthia Geppert write in an article titled "Physician-Assisted Suicide and the Autonomy Myth,"

> most statutes provide nothing remotely resembling "autonomy" for the patient, in either the procedural or personal sense. Patients who wish to avail themselves of prescribed, lethal medication must clear a number of procedural and administrative hurdles that depend entirely on the diagnostic, prognostic, and prescriptive authority of the patient's physician. The controlling decisions regarding the patient's diagnosis; the need for a consultant to confirm the diagnosis; the putative "terminal" nature of the illness; the completion of required certification forms; and, finally, the writing of the lethal prescription are all exercises of the physician's autonomy.
>
> Even refusals of a patient's request for PAS reinforce the primary role of physician autonomy in these decisions. It is clear that,

at any point in this sequence—i.e., prior to dispensing of the lethal drugs—a simple act on the part of the patient's physician could overturn the patient's request for assisted suicide…. In short, PAS provides no procedural autonomy for the candidate/patient. Rather, PAS legislation is an example of extreme heteronomy—i.e., handing over power and authority to others.[5]

It is not merely a matter of physicians rubber-stamping this decision-making process, either. In 1995, for example, 9,700 patients requested euthanasia in the Netherlands. Of those requests, only 3,200 were approved by the physicians.[6] Thus, in two out of every three cases physicians decided against the patients' will; the patients did not get to make the final decision. And while it is true that most jurisdictions in the US that have legalized assisted suicide require the patient to self-administer the deadly drug, still the patients must ask their physicians for the drug in the first place. This is hardly upholding the autonomy of the individual to decide if and when and how to die.

Interestingly, in jurisdictions that have legalized physician-administered euthanasia—such as the Netherlands and Belgium—most patients opt for the physician to kill them, rather than administering the drug themselves. Which raises questions: If autonomy is such a sacred matter, then why do others need to be involved so integrally in the process?[7] If autonomy is so important, why not commit suicide without assistance or official sanction? The need for someone to metaphorically hold one's hand through the process, the need for a stamp of approval on one's actions—these very human and understandable emotions suggest that "personal autonomy" might not be the value of highest importance to us.

And note another irony regarding the restrictions on assisted suicide: many on the political left, who are often more prone to promoting assisted suicide than are conservatives—and who frequently appeal to the autonomy argument in promoting assisted suicide—think that the powers of the state over the individual should increase, not decrease. This contradiction generally goes unremarked.

Influenced by Others

Jeanette Hall's change of heart also illustrates another problem with the autonomy argument. Humans are social beings and are influenced by their fellow humans, both for good and for ill. Not only did Dr. Stevens influence Hall's decision; he did so by reminding her of the social connections that she valued.

Conversely, in the years 1998 to 2002 over one-third of those requesting assisted suicide in Oregon reported that one reason affecting their decision to end their life was the feeling that they were a burden to family and friends.[8] Our social structures affect our decisions, as does the broader social context; in this way we are not wholly autonomous.

This is why "suicide contagion" exists. Suicide contagion—also called the Werther Effect—is such a well-known phenomenon that the World Health Organization and other organizations have published media guidelines about how to report on suicides. The increase of suicides in the wake of highly publicized suicides suggests that suicide is a decision strongly influenced by the deeds of others. It is not the decision of an isolated individual.

The media generally abides by these guidelines about reporting on suicides, with one major exception. When it comes to assisted suicide, they play by different rules. In 2014 a young twenty-nine-year-old woman, Brittany Maynard, who had a terminal illness, moved to Oregon to receive assisted suicide. She received abundant press coverage, mostly sympathizing with her request for assisted suicide, and much of it glorifying her for taking that step. There was a spike in requests for assisted suicide in Oregon that year, possibly the result of this positive publicity.[9]

People do not make decisions in a social vacuum. And for a decision as drastic as choosing death, surely we should surface and address the plain fact that often our opinions and our decisions are not truly ours, but merely a reflection of strong-minded social influencers around us. This leads, of course, to difficult questions about agency, which is distinct from decisional capacity.

Influenced by the Law

Further, the legalization and ensuing increased social acceptance of assisted suicide and euthanasia—or conversely, its prohibition and resulting lack of acceptance—influence whether or not people decide to pursue assisted suicide (or euthanasia). A common saying is "you can't legislate morality," but that is not entirely true. Laws don't merely reflect society; they also shape it. People tend to assume if something is illegal, it is bad. And when something that was once illegal becomes legal, it tends to signal to people that the formerly illegal activity is morally OK. The law thus serves a tutorial function.

At a training session for euthanasia providers in Canada, the speakers admitted that some euthanasia recipients were driven by socioeconomic circumstances to end their lives, but tragically, these speakers did not even suggest that euthanasia providers should try to dissuade people from killing themselves because of poverty.[10] As one euthanasia provider said, "As all Canadians have rights to an assisted death, people who are lonely or poor also have those rights." This attitude prevails even when a medical condition is not the reason for requesting death, but merely a way to "check a box" on a form.[11]

Sometimes, perversely, the government itself creates the conditions that funnel people into the assisted suicide pipeline. In 2022 in Ontario, Canada, a man with disabilities required long-term care. He wanted the government to assign him to a facility near his family, but the government refused. This man came to the conclusion that dying was preferable to living without his family nearby, and requested euthanasia. He was not eager to die, but he considered the conditions the government was imposing on him unbearable.[12] This is the reality, despite Justin Trudeau's assurance in 2019 that people could choose assisted death "in a way that isn't because you're not getting the supports and cares that you actually need."[13]

It is bad enough when people who feel neglected and abandoned ask for euthanasia or assisted suicide. It is even worse when government or medical personnel actually suggest euthanasia or assisted suicide as a way out of "difficulties." Two veterans, for instance, asked

Veterans Affairs Canada for assistance. One requested PTSD treatment, and the other wanted a wheelchair ramp. Instead, their case worker asked if they would like to apply for euthanasia.[14] Are such individuals likely to feel empowered by the "opportunity" presented to them, or railroaded into choosing death?

Pseudo-Autonomy

Advocates of assisted suicide and euthanasia often portray the autonomy of an individual to decide how he or she will die as liberating and rational. However, if we examine the reasons that individuals provide for requesting assisted suicide, we find a different picture. It is often an emotion-based decision, and those emotions are not necessarily grounded in objective reality and rational thinking.

Pies and Geppert point out that many seriously ill people experience "subtle cognitive distortions" that cloud their judgment and cause them to draw erroneous conclusions about their situation. They may say that "nobody understands" or "no one can help." Pies and Geppert write, "These distortions may respond favorably to cognitive behavioral interventions, which may avert or abort a request for PAS. (Importantly, no current PAS statutes require any form of psychotherapy for patients seeking to end their lives via PAS.)"[15]

Human emotion is a complicated and often obscure thing. Pies and Geppert note that "a request for assisted suicide may mask deeper, underlying wishes or fantasies—e.g., the request may be a covert plea for the physician to be more empathic about the patient's situation, or amount to a test of whether the physician still values the patient's life as death approaches."

"Crucially," Pies and Geppert say, "the evaluating physician typically has neither the training nor the tools to reliably and validly assess such complex and nuanced emotional states."[16]

In Canada, for instance, euthanasia providers are given checklists for assessing a patient's mental competency to make a decision to die. These lists are not binding, but are merely guidelines, and further are far too shallow to tease out conditions that tend to impair judgment, such as depression.[17]

When to Argue, When to Let Die

The question, of course, arises: why should euthanasia providers even attempt to screen out candidates lacking clear judgment?

On the one hand, "evidence suggests that when physicians intervene and successfully address issues such as pain, depression, and other medical problems, as many as 46% of patients seeking assisted suicide will change their minds."[18] On the other hand, physicians are urged to respect patients' self-determination, that is, their autonomy.

Which are they supposed to do? Save lives, or listen to patients who may—or may not—be capable of making fully informed, rational, uncoerced decisions?

The same question applies to suicide in general. Many government and private entities promote programs to dissuade most people from committing suicide (while simultaneously some states approve of those asking for assisted suicide). Suicide prevention hotlines provide counsel and support for those feeling depressed or anxious.

Thus, those governments that allow assisted suicide or euthanasia have become schizophrenic on the issue of suicide, campaigning against it, on the one hand, but accepting it in certain cases (decided not by the individual, but by the government) and even championing an individual's right to pursue it.

Is the idea that anyone "rational" enough to go to a physician for help in dying must in fact be capable of making a clear-headed decision? Whereas someone who chooses to die alone must be making an emotion-based and possibly incorrect decision? If so, this strikes yet another blow against the autonomy argument: you are only capable of self-determining when to die if you determine not to do it alone.

Personal Autonomy versus the Community

Another flaw in the autonomy argument is that it assumes that the only person's feelings to consider are those of the person seeking assisted suicide or euthanasia. What about the community, left behind to feel rejected, guilt-stricken, subject not to the natural ebb and flow of life and death, but to sudden, violent artificial removals?

What about physicians, many of whom went into medicine simply to heal others? They are being thrust into untenable positions, asked to make impossible life-or-death decisions, asked to kill. Many of them have profound misgivings about the wisdom and morality of the whole assisted suicide enterprise.[19] Indeed, some medical personnel have left palliative care because they can no longer care for patients in what they believe is an appropriate way, finding instead that "their function was reduced to preparing patient and their families for lethal injections."[20]

And what about family and friends? In a particularly poignant case, Simon Binner, a fifty-seven-year-old man suffering from a motor neuron disease, not only decided to travel to Switzerland to be killed at a euthanasia facility, but also publicized and glorified his decision in a BBC documentary, "How to Die: Simon's Choice." Many lauded his decision, but his wife and two children were devastated. His wife testified that "his death felt like abandonment." Further, she stated, "There was a sense of people saying, 'Hasn't he done a wonderful thing?' But I had two children who were in bits."[21]

Worse yet, in some cases families have been shocked to learn only after the fact that their loved ones died of voluntary euthanasia, their not having been informed at all beforehand. In a tragic case mentioned previously in these pages, an elderly Italian woman, who was physically and mentally healthy, traveled to Switzerland to kill herself, because she was upset that she had lost her beauty. Her family only learned about her plans when they were informed of her demise.[22]

The notion that one's life only matters to oneself is clearly faulty.

We Are Not Our Own

All the above considerations are sufficient to form a solid rational basis for rejecting the autonomy argument for the legalization of euthanasia and assisted suicide. But there is one additional problem with the autonomy argument: it is rooted in a materialistic worldview. This is the view that the natural world is all that exists, that we are therefore unconnected to anything spiritual beyond ourselves, that we are not beholden to a creator nor living under an ultimate lawgiver, and that therefore we are free to do as we please. Such a conclusion cannot be simply assumed, particularly as it goes against the conclusions of most people across time and place.

The argument to autonomy from materialism also saws off the limb it is sitting on, for if matter is all there is, then not only autonomy but agent freedom goes out the door. Both turn out to be an illusion, with each human person being nothing more, at root, than a collocation of atoms obeying the laws of physics and chemistry—meat robots if you will. If championing individual human liberty is the goal, embracing materialism is the absolute wrong way to go about it.

If, on the other hand, we are spiritual beings created by a wise and loving God, then we possess true agent freedom, even if our condition is characterized by the ties of community and culture rather than any imagined radical autonomy. And if such a God has created us—as He has—then our lives should be under his guidance. We did not create ourselves. We do not own our own bodies. We have a responsibility to obey our Creator and submit to his will and his timing for our death.

Obviously, those who dismiss or question the existence of God will not find this final argument compelling, but as I explain in greater depth in a brief e-book, *Made in the Image of God: Why Human Dignity Argues for a Creator*,[23] everyone, even some of the most strident atheists, seems to have a deep knowledge and intuition that human life has value. And if human life has value—as it does—then, as I argue in those pages, this implies that a Creator has imbued us with that value. Further, because God has created each one of us, every human being has equal and inherent value, including those with disabilities or terminal illnesses.

The Impossibility of Doing as We Please

The autonomy argument fails for many reasons. It fails to acknowledge that the death of the person choosing assisted suicide or euthanasia ends that person's autonomy. And it fails to acknowledge that each person's "autonomy" is heavily influenced by external forces and, in many cases, by irrational and fleeting internal factors. Governments who legalize assisted suicide and/or euthanasia never actually allow complete autonomy, but place stipulations on who can make the choice to die and, usually, elevate the decision-making power of authorities such as physicians over that of the patients. Finally, the autonomy argument rests on a materialistic foundation—which, for matters of life and death, as for matters of personal and societal well-being in general, is a shaky foundation indeed.

Conclusion:
Redefining Death
with Dignity

I N THE PAST COUPLE OF CENTURIES, ESPECIALLY IN THE PAST FEW
decades, attitudes toward assisted suicide and euthanasia have shift-
ed considerably in Western culture. Until the late twentieth century
the influence of the Judeo-Christian worldview in Western culture
was strong enough to keep these practices taboo and illegal. According to the Judeo-Christian understanding, human life is intrinsically
valuable, regardless of a person's physical and intellectual capacities.

Further, the Judeo-Christian tradition has always considered it
one of the highest moral imperatives to "love your neighbor as yourself." This means sacrificing one's own time, energy, and resources
for the sake of others. This ethical command to love others includes
those with disabilities or diseases. Jesus here led by example. He laid
healing hands on the crippled, the blind, the hemorrhaging, the psychologically tormented or demon-possessed, the lepers—all manner
of sufferers, those most desperate and lonely and in despair. And he
explicitly commanded his disciples to do the same. He stated, "When
you give a dinner or a supper, do not ask your friends, your brothers,
your relatives, nor rich neighbors, lest they also invite you back, and
you be repaid. But when you give a feast, invite the poor, the maimed,
the lame, the blind. And you will be blessed, because they cannot
repay you; for you shall be repaid at the resurrection of the just."[1]

This attitude of love and compassion toward those with physical and mental ailments and disabilities—true compassion that welcomes them into our lives—is crucial in combatting the temptation toward suicide that many sufferers feel. Recall that various surveys of people seeking euthanasia and assisted suicide have shown that loneliness is a significant factor. For instance, in the 2021 Canadian report about the reasons that people sought medical assistance in dying (MAiD), 17.3 percent (thus about 1,721 people) listed loneliness as a key factor.[2] Rosina Kamis, a Canadian who died by assisted suicide in 2021, said, "I think if more people cared about me, I might be able to handle the suffering caused by my physical illnesses alone…. Sometimes all the pain will go away just by having another human being here."[3] Even the Surgeon General of the US, Vivek H. Murthy, warned in 2023 of the negative health impacts of loneliness, which he described as an epidemic.[4]

Conversely, other studies have shown that people with strong family and social networks are less inclined to ask for assisted suicide. Forging loving relationships in families and among friends—and expanding our circles of care outward to encompass those who are lonely and vulnerable—is crucial to creating a society where we all can live and die with dignity.

Offering people an "easy way" to end their lives does not let them "die with dignity." Superficially it may seem compassionate to some. However, in reality it tells them they are no longer worth helping, that they are nothing but the sum of their aches and pains, their fears and their despair.

This is not dignifying. It is demeaning.

No, the proponents of killing the sufferer should not be allowed to twist and co-opt the idea of "dying with dignity."

The only way to create a culture of truly good death—death with dignity—is for us to continue to uphold the sanctity and value of all human life.

All humans are equal, regardless of their disability or disease. We should never succumb to the temptation to think that some people's lives are so valueless that we should help them kill themselves. It is far better to offer people love and compassion than help in ending their lives.

This is not easy and will involve sacrifices, but loving our neighbors as ourselves has always required courage and self-denial. Let's choose to be courageous and compassionate as we help people choose life rather than death.

ENDNOTES

INTRODUCTION

1. Joni Eareckson and Joe Musser, *Joni* (Grand Rapids, MI: Zondervan, 1976), 48–49, 74–75.

2. There are a wide variety of situations where steps are not taken to save a life. Consider the differences among the following cases: an EMT who does not perform CPR on a ninety-year-old who has signed a "do not resuscitate" request and is suffering from terminal cancer; a doctor who refuses to perform the Heimlich maneuver on the diner choking at the neighboring table; and a son hoping to inherit wealth who allows his father to drown in a swimming pool. Some instances fall into the category of "passive euthanasia" or even criminal negligence while others do not. The word "euthanasia" implies the intentional ending of a life. Conceding that we cannot stave off death forever and allowing nature to take its course (rather than choosing to prolong the act of dying) does not constitute euthanasia, passive or otherwise. Death can be expected or foreseen without being intended. For an in-depth discussion of the importance of intent, see Iain Brassington, "What Passive Euthanasia Is," *BMC Medical Ethics* 21 (May 14, 2020), https://bmcmedethics.biomedcentral.com/articles/10.1186/s12910-020-00481-7.

3. The idea that it is legitimate for a physician to provide palliative care that likely—but unintentionally—will shorten the patient's life is known as the doctrine of double effect.

4. For a table of nations and their laws regarding euthanasia and assisted suicide, see Nicola Davis, "What's the Difference Between Euthanasia, Assisted Dying, and Assisted Suicide?," *Guardian*, July 15, 2019, https://www.theguardian.com/news/2019/jul/15/euthanasia-and-assisted-dying-rates-are-soaring-but-where-are-they-legal. See also "Where Is Euthanasia Legal?," *World Population Review*, 2024, https://worldpopulationreview.com/country-rankings/where-is-euthanasia-legal.

5. Yuval Noah Harari, *Sapiens: A Brief History of Humankind* (New York: Harper, 2015), 109.

6. Richard Weikart, *Made in the Image of God: Why Human Dignity Argues for a Creator* (Lafayette, IN: Ratio Christi Press, 2022), available at https://press.ratiochristi.org/product/are-you-the-image-of-god/.

1. The Devaluation of Life in Classical Antiquity

1. Nick Vujicic, *Life without Limits: Inspiration for a* Ridiculously *Good Life* (New York: Doubleday, 2010), vii–viii.

2. Vujicic, *Life without Limits*, 2.

3. "The Oath of Hippocrates," in *The Right to Die Debate: A Documentary History*, ed. Marjorie B. Zucker (Westport, CN: Greenwood Press, 1999), 240.

4. Steven H. Miles, *The Hippocratic Oath and the Ethics of Medicine* (Oxford, UK: Oxford University Press, 2004), 71–73.

5. Paul Carrick, *Medical Ethics in Antiquity: Philosophical Perspectives on Abortion and Euthanasia* (Dordrecht, The Netherlands: D. Reidel Publishing, 1985), 155–156.

6. Miles, *The Hippocratic Oath*, 3–4.

7. Edward J. Larson and Darrel Amundsen, *A Different Death: Euthanasia and the Christian Tradition* (Downers Grove, IL: InterVarsity Press, 1998), 34–35.

8. Carrick, *Medical Ethics in Antiquity*, 134.

9. Plato, excerpt from *Phaedo*, in *The Ethics of Suicide: Historical Sources*, ed. Margaret Pabst Battin (Oxford, UK: Oxford University Press, 2015), 76.

10. Plato, *The Republic*, Book 3, http://classics.mit.edu/Plato/republic.mb.txt.

11. Plato, excerpt from *The Laws*, in *The Ethics of Suicide: Historical Sources*, 83.

12. Aristotle, *Nicomachean Ethics*, http://classics.mit.edu/Aristotle/nicomachaen.mb.txt.

13. Judith Evans Grubbs, "Infant Exposure and Infanticide," in *The Oxford Handbook of Childhood and Education in the Classical World*, ed. Judith Evans Grubbs and Tim Parkin (Oxford, UK: Oxford University Press, 2013), 88.

14. Grubbs, "Infant Exposure and Infanticide," 83–88.

15. Reported by the ancient Greek biographer Diogenes Laërtius, *The Lives and Opinions of Eminent Philosophers*, trans. C. D. Yonge (London: G. Bell and Sons, 1915), Book 7, 271, https://www.gutenberg.org/files/57342/57342-h/57342-h.htm.

16. Laërtius, *The Lives and Opinions of Eminent Philosophers*, Book 7, 326.

17. Chrysippus, "The Stoics' Five Reasons for Suicide," in *The Ethics of Suicide: Historical Sources*, 91.

18. Seneca, *Ad Lucilium Epistulae Morales*, trans. Richard M. Gummere, 3 vols. (New York: G. P. Putnam's Sons: William Heinemann, 1962), 2:70.

19. Seneca, "On Anger," *Moral Essays*, trans. John W. Basore (London: Heinemann, 1928), 295. Available at *Sophia Project*, 38, http://www.sophia-project.org/uploads/1/3/9/5/13955288/seneca_anger.pdf.

20. Seneca, *Ad Lucilium Epistulae Morales*, 2:70.

21. Lucretius, *On the Nature of Things*. Quoted in Jennifer Michael Hecht, *Stay: A History of Suicide and the Philosophies against It* (New Haven, CT: Yale University Press, 2013), 35.

22. Seneca, "On Anger," *Sophia Project*, 8.

23. Emiel Eyben, "Family Planning in Graeco-Roman Antiquity," *Ancient Society* 11/12 (1980/1981): 16, https://www.jstor.org/stable/44080042.

24. The Hebrew nation dates back to the second millennium BCE, though the Hebrews were often under the rule of others, including the Babylonians, Assyrians, and Greeks. At the time of Jesus, the Hebrews were under Roman rule.

25. Judges 9:50–56. Here and elsewhere in these pages, the translation cited is the New King James Version. Similarly, a badly injured King Saul (who because of ongoing disobedience had lost divine approval) had his armor-bearer kill him to avoid capture by his enemies (I Samuel 31); and King Zimri, facing overthrow, "went into the citadel of the king's house and burned the king's house down upon himself with fire, and died, because of the sins which he had committed in doing evil in the sight of the Lord," (I Kings 16:18b–19a). There is one instance of a royal adviser (Ahithophel, in II Samuel 16–17) committing suicide because the king chose to ignore his advice. And there is the story of Samson, who died when he dislodged the pillars holding up the roof—but it appears that Samson's goal was to kill his enemies, and his own death was incidental. And in any case Samson is described as committing a long list of follies (Judges 16).

26. Job 2:9–10.

27. James 5:11.

28. The only account of this event comes from Josephus, a Jew raised in Jerusalem. Historians believe he based his account on Roman field commentaries. See Flavius Josephus, *The Wars of the Jews* [78 AD], trans. William Whiston (1951), Book 7, chap. 9, https://www.gutenberg.org/files/2850/2850-h/2850-h.htm#link32HCH0008.

29. "Issues in Jewish Ethics: Suicide," *Jewish Virtual Library*, accessed February 2024, https://www.jewishvirtuallibrary.org/suicide-in-judaism.

30. Josephus, *The Wars of the Jews,* Book 3, chap. 8, par. 5.

31. Josephus, *The Wars of the Jews,* Book 3, chap. 8, par. 5.

32. Josephus, *The Wars of the Jews,* Book 3, chap. 8, par. 5.

33. Josephus, it should be noted, failed to convince his peers. He then suggested (at least according to his account) a method by which they drew lots and killed each other; Josephus was one of two left standing at the end. Josephus, *The Wars of the Jews,* Book 3, chap. 8, par. 7. In mathematics this incident has resulted in a theoretical problem known as the "Josephus Problem." See "Josephus Problem," *Wikipedia*, last modified January 12, 2024, https://en.wikipedia.org/wiki/Josephus_problem.

34. Shlomo Minkowitz, "Suicide in Judaism," *Chabad*, accessed February 2024, https://www.chabad.org/library/article_cdo/aid/4372311/jewish/Suicide-in-Judaism.htm.

35. Byron L. Sherwin, "Jewish Views on Euthanasia," in *Last Rights? Assisted Suicide and Euthanasia Debated*, ed. Michael M. Uhlmann (Washington, DC: Ethics and Public Policy Center, 1998), chap. 7.

36. Caius Cornelius Tacitus, *The Histories* [circa 100–110 AD], trans. W. Hamilton Fyfe (Oxford, UK: Clarendon Press, 1912), Book 5, par. 5, https://www.gutenberg.org/files/16927/16927-h/16927-h.htm.

37. Flavius Josephus, *Against Apion* [circa 94 CE], trans. William Whiston (1895), Book 2, par. 25, https://www.gutenberg.org/files/2849/2849-h/2849-h.htm. Modern Judaism is not univocal on this. See Fred Rosner, "The Beginning of Life in

Judaism," *My Jewish Learning*, accessed February 2024, https://www.myjewishlearning.com/article/the-beginning-of-life-in-judaism/.

38. Larson and Amundsen, *A Different Death*, esp. chap. 2 and 3.

39. Matthew 27:5.

40. I Corinthians 3:16–17; 6:19–20.

41. Ephesians 5:29.

42. Hebrews 12:5–11.

43. James 5:14–15.

44. 2 Corinthians 12:7–10.

45. John 16:33.

46. Matthew 18:1–6, 10–14; Matthew 19:13–14.

47. Luke 14:14.

48. Larson and Amundsen, *A Different Death*, 103.

49. Justin Martyr, excerpt from *The Second Apology*, in *The Ethics of Suicide: Historical Sources*, ed. Margaret Pabst Battin (Oxford, UK: Oxford University Press, 2015), 151.

50. Larson and Amundsen, *A Different Death*, 84, 114.

51. Eusebius, *Church History*, Book 8, chap. 12, available at *New Advent*, http://www.newadvent.org/fathers/250108.htm.

52. *Didache*, chap. 2, available at *Early Christian Writings*, https://www.earlychristianwritings.com/text/didache-roberts.html.

53. O. M. Bakke, *When Children Became People: The Birth of Childhood in Early Christianity* (Minneapolis: Fortress Press, 2005), 114–124.

54. Christian Laes, "Raising a Disabled Child," in *The Oxford Handbook of Childhood and Education in the Classical World*, 138.

55. Judith Evans Grubbs, "Infant Exposure and Infanticide," in *The Oxford Handbook of Childhood and Education in the Classical World*, 98.

56. Augustine, *City of God*, Book 1, chap. 17–27, available at *Christian Classical Ethereal Library*, https://www.ccel.org/ccel/schaff/npnf102.

57. Augustine, *City of God*, Book 1, chap. 26.

58. Thomas Aquinas, *Summa Theologica*, Second Part of the Second Part, Question 64, Article 5, http://www.documentacatholicaomnia.eu/03d/1225-1274,_Thomas_Aquinas,_Summa_Theologiae_%5B1%5D,_EN.pdf.

59. Georges Minois, *History of Suicide: Voluntary Death in Western Culture*, trans. Lydia G. Cochrane (Baltimore, MA: Johns Hopkins University Press, 1999), 9, 37.

2. Renaissance and Enlightenment

1. Martin Luther, excerpt from *Table Talk* [1566], in *The Ethics of Suicide: Historical Sources*, ed. Margaret Pabst Battin (Oxford, UK: Oxford University Press, 2015), 244.

2. John Calvin, excerpt from *Sermons on Job* [1554–1555], in *The Ethics of Suicide*, ed. Margaret Pabst Battin, 249–252.

3. R. V. Young, "*Sic est in Republica:* Utopian Ideology and the Misreading of Thomas More," *Humanitas* 26 (2013): 75–93.

4. Thomas More, "Of Their Slaves and of Their Marriages," in *Utopia* [1516], https://www.gutenberg.org/files/2130/2130-h/2130-h.htm.

5. Paul D. Green, "Suicide, Martyrdom and Thomas More," *Studies in the Renaissance* 19 (1972): 135–155, esp. 142–144.

6. Michel de Montaigne, "A Custom of the Isle of Cea," in *The Ethics of Suicide: Historical Sources*, ed. Margaret Pabst Battin (Oxford, UK: Oxford University Press, 2015), 280–284.

7. Georges Minois, *History of Suicide: Voluntary Death in Western Culture*, trans. Lydia G. Cochrane (Baltimore, MA: Johns Hopkins University Press, 1999), 92.

8. Minois, *History of Suicide*, 106.

9. Minois, *History of Suicide*, 64–66, 86, 106–107.

10. William Shakespeare, *Hamlet*, Act 3, Scene 1, 127, https://www.folgerdigitaltexts.org/download/pdf/Ham.pdf.

11. William Shakespeare, *Hamlet*, Act 5, Scene 1.

12. As a deterrent, for many centuries the Catholic church did not allow religious burials for those who committed suicide, though after 1614 an exception was made for insanity. (*Hamlet*, set in medieval Denmark, was written sometime between 1599 and 1601). See Stanislaw Adamiak and Jan Dohnalik, "The Prohibition of Suicide and Its Theological Rationale in Catholic Moral and Theological Tradition: Origins and Development," *Journal of Religion and Health* 62, no. 6 (August 2023), https://www.ncbi.nlm.nih.gov/pmc/articles/PMC10682050/. In the 1980s, the ban on funerals for suicides was removed. But Ranana Leigh Dine notes, "The Church was able to drop its restrictions on funerals since suicide was seen as an act beyond the control of the deceased and thus worthy of mercy and compassion. In cases of physician-assisted dying, the patient must have consciously and willingly agreed to the procedure, undermining this understanding of suicide." Dine, "You Shall Bury Him: Burial, Suicide, and the Development of Catholic Law and Theology," *Medical Humanities* 46, no. 3 (September 2020): 299–310.

13. *Biathanatos*, from the Greek, meaning "violent death."

14. John Donne, *Biathanatos* [1608], eds. Michael Rudick and M. Pabst Battin (New York: Garland, 1982), 39–40, 42, https://web.archive.org/web/20111117203143/http://www.philosophy.utah.edu/onlinepublications/PDFs/Biathanatos_CompleteText.pdf.

15. John Bunyan, *Pilgrim's Progress* [1678] (Desiring God: Minneapolis, MN: 2014), 129–130, https://document.desiringgod.org/the-pilgrim-s-progress-en.pdf?ts=1446648353.

16. Voltaire, *The Works of Voltaire: A Contemporary Version*, vol. 7, trans. William F. Fleming (Paris: E. R. DuMont, 1901), 25. Voltaire gets a few details wrong in relating this story, but the gist of it is accurate.

17. Michael MacDonald and Terence R. Murphy, *Sleepless Souls: Suicide in Early Modern England* (Oxford, UK: Clarendon Press, 1990), 157.

18. Claire Hopkins, *Trinity: 450 Years of an Oxford College Community* (Oxford UP, 2005), 194.

19. Minois, *History of Suicide*, 179.

20. Stephen Lalor and Matthew Tindal, *Freethinker: An Eighteenth-Century Assault on Religion* (London: Continuum, 2006), 27.

21. S. E. Sprott, *The English Debate on Suicide from Donne to Hume* (La Salle, IL: Open Court, 1961), 71–85, 96–97, quote at 78.

22. MacDonald and Murphy, *Sleepless Souls*, 2, 5–6.

23. For a good, brief discussion of Radicati, see Jonathan I. Israel, *Radical Enlightenment: Philosophy and the Making of Modernity 1650–1750* (Oxford, UK: Oxford University Press, 2001), 68–69.

24. Alberto Radicati di Passerano, *A Philosophical Dissertation upon Death* (London: W. Mears, 1732), 5.

25. Radicati, *A Philosophical Dissertation upon Death*, 5–11, quotes at 10, 11.

26. Radicati, *A Philosophical Dissertation upon Death*, 29–84; quotes at 61, 81, 70.

27. Radicati, *A Philosophical Dissertation upon Death*, 86–93.

28. Lester G. Crocker, "The Discussion of Suicide in the Eighteenth Century," *Journal of the History of Ideas* 13, no. 1 (1952): 47–72. Minois, *History of Suicide*, chap. 8–10.

29. Charles Louis de Secondat de Montesquieu, *Persian Letters*, vol. 2, trans. John Ozell (London: J. Tonson, 1736), 9–12.

30. Charles Louis de Secondat de Montesquieu, *Persian Letters* (London: Athenaeum Publishing, 1897), 144; Minois, *History of Suicide*, 228.

31. Voltaire, "Cato on Suicide, and the Abbe St. Cyran's Book Legitimating Suicide," in *The Works of Voltaire: A Contemporary Version*, vol. 7, trans. William F. Fleming (Paris: E. R. DuMont, 1901), 20.

32. Voltaire, "Cato on Suicide, and the Abbe St. Cyran's Book Legitimating Suicide," 20, 23, quote at 27.

33. Voltaire, "Cato on Suicide, and the Abbe St. Cyran's Book Legitimating Suicide," 31–32.

34. Baron D'Holbach, *The System of Nature*, trans. H. D. Robinson (New York: G. W. and A. J. Matsell, 1836), 136–37, 348–349; quotes at 137.

35. Minois, *History of Suicide*, 253.

36. MacDonald and Murphy, *Sleepless Souls*, 160.

37. *Last Rights? Assisted Suicide and Euthanasia Debated*, ed. Michael M. Uhlmann (Washington, DC: Ethics and Public Policy Center, 1998), 37.

38. David Hume, "On Suicide" [1755], in *Life, Death and Meaning: Key Philosophical Readings on the Big Questions*, ed. David Benatar (Lanham, MD: Rowman and Littlefield Publishers, 2004), 289–293; quotations at 292 and 293.

39. Hume, "On Suicide," in *Life, Death and Meaning*, 292.

40. Hume, "On Suicide," in *Life, Death and Meaning*, 294–295.

41. Immanuel Kant, "Grounding for the Metaphysics of Morals" [1785], in *The Ethics of Suicide: Historical Sources*, ed. Margaret Pabst Battin (Oxford, UK: Oxford University Press, 2015), 425–427.

42. Immanuel Kant, "Lectures on Ethics," in *The Ethics of Suicide*, 429.

43. Kant, "Lectures on Ethics," in *The Ethics of Suicide*, 431.

44. Kant, "Lectures on Ethics," in *The Ethics of Suicide*, 432.

3. Euthanasia Meets Eugenics

1. The child was missing an ear; had a defective development of skin over the shoulders that made the neck look short; had a fusion of the kidneys; had a missing coccyx; and had a closure at the end of the intestines (he needed an artificial anus, and it was this that led to his death). See John Dill Robertson, "The Case of the Bollinger Baby," *Journal of the American Medical Association* 23 (December 4, 1915), available at https://jamanetwork.com/journals/jama/article-abstract/447318. See also "Jury Clears, Yet Condemns Dr. Haiselden," *Chicago Daily Tribune*, November 20, 1915, available at *Disability Museum*, https://www.disabilitymuseum.org/dhm/lib/detail.html?id=1236&page=all.

2. Martin S. Pernick, *The Black Stork: Eugenics and the Death of "Defective" Babies in American Medicine and Motion Pictures since 1915* (New York: Oxford University Press, 1996), 3–5, 11, quote at 144.

3. Mary Waller, "The Tragic Case of Baby Bollinger," *Jane Addams Papers Project*, July 18, 2018, janeaddams.ramapo.edu/2018/07/the-tragic-case-of-baby-bollinger/.

4. Robertson, "The Case of the Bollinger Baby."

5. Pernick, *Black Stork*, 83–84, 96.

6. Waller, "The Tragic Case of Baby Bollinger."

7. *Pernick, Black Stork*, 97.

8. Pernick, *Black Stork*, 85–87; quotes at 95.

9. Michael Stolberg, "Two Pioneers of Euthanasia around 1800," *Hastings Center Report* 38, no. 3 (2008): 19–22.

10. Ian Dowbiggin, *A Merciful End: The Euthanasia Movement in Modern America* (Oxford, UK: Oxford University Press, 2003), 2.

11. Dowbiggin, *Merciful End*, 2, 8.

12. N. D. A. Kemp, *"Merciful Release": The History of the British Euthanasia Movement* (Manchester: Manchester University Press, 2002), 3, quote at 19.

13. Hans-Walter Schmuhl, *Rassenhygiene, Nationalsozialismus, Euthanasie: Von der Verhütung zur Vernichtung 'lebensunwerten Lebens' 1890–1945* (Göttingen: Vandenhoek und Ruprecht, 1987), 18–19, quote at 106.

14. I provide many concrete examples of these points in my earlier books, *The Death of Humanity: And the Case for Life* (Washington, DC: Regnery Faith, 2016) and *From Darwin to Hitler: Evolutionary Ethics, Eugenics, and Racism in Germany* (New York: Palgrave Macmillan, 2004).

15. Quoted in Lionel A. Tollemache, *Stones of Stumbling* (London: William Rice, 1893), 8.

16. Quoted in Ian Dowbiggin, *A Concise History of Euthanasia: Life, Death, God, and Medicine* (Lanham, MD: Rowman and Littlefield, 2005), 51.

17. Good discussions of Williams' essay are in: Dowbiggin, *Concise History of Euthanasia*, 49–51; and Kemp, *"Merciful Release,"* 11–21.

18. Lionel A. Tollemache, "The Cure for Incurables," in *Stones of Stumbling* (London: William Rice, 1893), quote at 20–21.

19. Kemp, *"Merciful Release,"* 27.

20. F. H. Bradley, "Some Remarks on Punishment," *International Journal of Ethics* 4 (1894): 269–284; quotations at 272, 280, 281, 283–284.

21. Ernst Haeckel, *Natürliche Schöpfungsgeschichte*, 2nd ed. (Berlin, 1870), 152–155; quote at 155.

22. Ernst Haeckel, *Die Lebenswunder: Gemeinverständliche Studien über Biologische Philosophie* (Stuttgart: Alfred Kröner, 1904), 21–22, 134–136.

23. Haeckel, *Lebenswunder*, 128–132.

24. Friedrich Nietzsche, "The Genealogy of Morals: An Attack," in *The Birth of Tragedy and The Genealogy of Morals*, trans. Francis Golffing (Garden City, NY: Doubleday Anchor, 1956), Essay 2, 210.

25. Nietzsche, *Will to Power*, part 872, quoted in Jean Gayon, "Nietzsche and Darwin," in *Biology and the Foundation of Ethics*, ed. Jane Maienschein and Michael Ruse (Cambridge, UK: Cambridge University Press, 1999), 183.

26. Nietzsche, "Also sprach Zarathustra," in *Werke in Drei Bänden*, ed. Karl Schlechta (Munich: Carl Hanser, 1966), Part 1, "Vom freien Tod," vol. 2, 333–336.

27. Friedrich Nietzsche, *Twilight of the Idols*, in *The Portable Nietzsche*, ed. and trans. Walter Kaufmann (New York: Penguin, 1976), 536–537.

28. Friedrich Nietzsche, "Die fröhliche Wissenschaft," in *Werke in Drei Bänden*, ed. Karl Schlechta (Munich: Carl Hanser, 1966), vol. 2, 84–85.

29. Adolf Jost, *Das Recht auf den Tod. Sociale Studie* (Göttingen: Dieterich'sche Verlagsbuchhandlung, 1895), 11–13, 47, and passim; quote at 11.

30. Udo Benzenhöfer, *Der gute Tod? Euthanasie und Sterbehilfe in Geschichte und Gegenwart* (Munich: C. H. Beck, 1999), 93, 233, n. 5.

31. Roland Gerkan, "Euthanasie," *Das monistische Jahrhundert* 2 (1913): 169–174.

32. Wilhelm Ostwald, "Euthanasie," *Monistische Jahrhundert* 2 (1913): 337–341.

33. I. van der Sluis, "The Movement for Euthanasia, 1875–1975," *Janus* 66 (1979): 136.

34. Bruce Fye, "Active Euthanasia: An Historical Survey of Its Conceptual Origins and Introduction into Medical Thought," *Bulletin of the History of Medicine* 52 (1978): 500.

35. Charles F. Deems, "Editor's Note," *Christian Thought: Lectures and Papers on Philosophy, Christian Evidence, Biblical Elucidation*, vol. 9 (New York: Wilbur B. Ketcham, 1891–92), 234–235.

36. Robert G. Ingersoll et al., *Is Suicide a Sin?: Robert G. Ingersoll's Famous Letter* (New York: Standard Publishing, 1894), 14–15, 22, 59, passim.

37. Jacob Appel, "A Duty to Kill? A Duty to Die? Rethinking the Euthanasia Controversy of 1906," *Bulletin of the History of Medicine* 78 (2004): 610–634; quotations at 610, 615.

38. Dowbiggin, *Merciful End*, 20.

39. Van der Sluis, "The Movement for Euthanasia," 137; see also Dowbiggin, *Concise History of Euthanasia*, 67–68; and Dowbiggin, *Merciful End*, 22.

40. Dowbiggin, *Merciful End*, 1.

4. Euthanasia Gains Ground in the US and Britain

1. Denise D. Knight, "The Dying of Charlotte Perkins Gilman," *American Transcendentalist Quarterly* (1999): 137–139.

2. Charlotte Perkins Gilman, "Suicide Note," *The Ethics of Suicide Digital Archive*, accessed February 20, 2024, ethicsofsuicide.lib.utah.edu/selections/charlotte -perkins-gilman/.

3. Charlotte Perkins Gilman, *His Religion and Hers: A Study of the Faith of Our Fathers and the Work of Our Mothers* (New York: Century, 1923), 10–11, 94, 193–194, 236, 272; quotations at 57, 246, 86, 274.

4. Charlotte Perkins Gilman, excerpt from *The Living of Charlotte Perkins Gilman: An Autobiography*, at *The Ethics of Suicide Digital Archive*, accessed April 9, 2020, ethicsofsuicide.lib.utah.edu/selections/charlotte-perkins-gilman/.

5. Charlotte Perkins Gilman, "Euthanasia Again," *Forerunner* 3 (October 1912): 262–263.

6. Charlotte Perkins Gilman, "Good and Bad Taste in Suicide," *Forerunner* 3 (May 1912): 130.

7. Martha J. Cutter, "The Writer as Doctor: New Models of Medical Discourse in Charlotte Perkins Gilman's Later Fiction," *Literature and Medicine* 20, no. 2 (Fall 2001): 176.

8. Charlotte Perkins Gilman, "The Right to Die," *The Forum and Century* 94, no. 5 (November 1935): 297–300.

9. Charles Francis Potter, *The Preacher and I: An Autobiography* (New York: Crown Publishers, 1951), 396–398.

10. Ian Dowbiggin, *A Merciful End: The Euthanasia Movement in Modern America* (Oxford, UK: Oxford University Press, 2003), 33.

11. Potter, *The Preacher and I*, 396.

12. Potter, *The Preacher and I*, 397–398.

13. Hereditarianists believe genetic makeup determines character traits such as intelligence, personality, and morality. In the "nature versus nurture" debate, they lean heavily and sometimes exclusively towards nature holding sway.

14. Mark Aldrich, "Progressive Economists and Scientific Racism: Walter Willcox and Black Americans, 1895–1910," *Phylon* 40, no. 1 (1979): 1–14.

15. The list of original board members is in Potter, *The Preacher and I*, 397–398.

16. Foster Kennedy, "The Problem of Social Control of the Congenital Defective: Education, Sterilization, Euthanasia," *American Journal of Psychiatry* 99 (1942): 13–16; quotes at 13, 14.

17. Dowbiggin, *A Merciful End*, 59–60.

18. Ian Dowbiggin, "'A Prey on Normal People': C. Killick Millard and the Euthanasia Movement in Great Britain, 1930–1955," *Journal of Contemporary History* 36 (2001): 75.

19. Dowbiggin, *A Merciful End*, 74.

20. Potter, *The Preacher and I*, 399.

21. "Resolution of the New York State Medical Society (1950)," in *The Right to Die Debate: A Documentary History,* ed. Marjorie B. Zucker (Westport, CN: Greenwood Press, 1999), 52.

22. "The Right to Kill," *Time* 26, no. 21 (November 18, 1935): 59.

23. Alexis Carrel, "The Mystery of Death," in *Medicine and Mankind: Lectures to the Laity Delivered at the Academy of Medicine of New York,* ed. Iago Galdston (New York: D. Appleton-Century, 1936), 215–216.

24. Andres Horacio Reggiani, *God's Eugenicist: Alexis Carrel and the Sociobiology of Decline* (New York: Berghahn Books, 2007), 70.

25. Alexis Carrel, *Man the Unknown* (New York: Harper and Brothers, 1935), 296, 298, 300, 318–319.

26. N. D. A. Kemp, *"Merciful Release": The History of the British Euthanasia Movement* (Manchester: Manchester University Press, 2002), 61–62, 73, quote at 66.

27. Kemp, *"Merciful Release,"* 83–86; Dowbiggin, "'A Prey on Normal People,'" 63–69.

28. Dowbiggin, "'A Prey on Normal People,'" 69–70.

29. Kemp, *"Merciful Release,"* 88–89.

30. Janet Lyon, "On the Asylum Road with Woolf and Mew," *Modernism* 18, no. 3 (2012): 558.

31. Havelock Ellis, *On Life and Sex: Essays of Love and Virtue,* vol. 2 (London: Wm. Heinemann, 1948), 251.

32. Ellis, *On Life and Sex,* 251–252.

33. Arthur Calder-Marshall, *Havelock Ellis* (London: Rupert Hart-Davis, 1959), 275.

34. Calder-Marshall, *Havelock Ellis,* 275–280.

35. "Voluntary Euthanasia (Legalisation) Bill [H. L.]," Parliament, United Kingdom, *Lords Hansard* Series 5 vol. 103 (December 1936): 468, https://api.parliament.uk/historic-hansard/lords/1936/dec/01/voluntary-euthanasia-legalisation-bill-hl#S5LV0103P0_19361201_HOL_8.

36. "Voluntary Euthanasia (Legalisation) Bill [H. L.]," 486–489.

37. "Voluntary Euthanasia (Legalisation) Bill [H. L.]," 502.

38. C. Killick Millard, "Correspondence," *British Medical Journal* (December 21, 1940): 881; at https://www-ncbi-nlm-nih-gov.libproxy.csustan.edu/pmc/articles/PMC2180139/pdf/brmedj04124-0029a.pdf.

39. Kemp, *"Merciful Release,"* chap. 5.

40. Dowbiggin, *A Merciful End,* 92.

41. Dowbiggin, *A Concise History of Euthanasia: Life, Death, God, and Medicine* (Lanham, MD: Rowman and Littlefield, 2005), 98.

42. Albert R. Jonsen, *The Birth of Bioethics* (New York: Oxford University Press, 1998), 41; Dowbiggin, *A Concise History of Euthanasia,* 105–106.

43. "Situation ethics" is the position that what is moral depends significantly on context or circumstances, with the goal being to behave lovingly and encourage harmony.

44. Joseph Fletcher, *Memoir of an Ex-Radical,* ed. Kenneth Vaux (Louisville: Westminster/John Knox, 1993), 58–59, 62–63, 76–77.

45. Fletcher, *Memoir of an Ex-Radical*, 82–85.

46. Joseph Fletcher, *Morals and Medicine* (London: Victor Gollancz Limited, 1955), chap. 7.

47. Joseph Fletcher, *Humanhood: Essays in Biomedical Ethics* (Buffalo: Prometheus Books, 1979), 135, 12–16, 144; see also 10–11.

48. Fletcher, *Humanhood*, 155, 146.

49. Fletcher, *Memoir of an Ex-Radical*, 87.

50. Kemp, *"Merciful Release,"* 147.

51. C. Killick Millard, "Correspondence," *British Medical Journal* (December 23, 1950): 1447.

52. Kemp, *"Merciful Release,"* 149.

53. Kemp, *"Merciful Release,"* 163.

54. Traditionally many Catholics have held that unbaptized infants who die go to Limbo, a place distinct from hell and by no means necessarily unpleasant. According to the Baltimore catechism, an influential catechism in the United States at the time Williams was making his arguments, "Infants who die without baptism of any kind do not suffer the punishment of those who die in mortal sin. They may enjoy a certain natural happiness, but they will not enjoy the supernatural happiness of heaven." The more recent Catechism of the Catholic Church takes a still more hopeful view, stating that "as regards children who have died without Baptism, the Church can only entrust them to the mercy of God, as she does in her funeral rites for them. Indeed, the great mercy of God who desires that all men should be saved, and Jesus' tenderness toward children which caused him to say: 'Let the children come to me, do not hinder them,' allow us to hope that there is a way of salvation for children who have died without Baptism." *Catechism of the Catholic Church: Second Edition* (1994), 1261, https://www.usccb.org/sites/default /files/flipbooks/catechism/323/.

55. Glanville Williams, *The Sanctity of Life and the Criminal Law* (New York: Alfred Knopf, 1970), 313, 15–16, 196, ix.

56. For a discussion of Bentham's position, see Richard Weikart, *The Death of Humanity: And the Case for Life* (Washington, DC: Regnery Faith, 2016), 166–169.

57. Williams, *The Sanctity of Life and the Criminal Law*, 18, 3, 22, 19.

58. Williams, *The Sanctity of Life and the Criminal Law*, 316–317.

5. Nazis Target "Life Unworthy of Life"

1. Bettina Winter, "Die Geschichte der NS-'Euthanasie'-Anstalt Hadamar," in *Verlegt nach Hadamar: Die Geschichte einer NS-"Euthanasie"-Anstalt*, ed. Bettina Winter (Kassel: Landeswohlfahrtsverbandes Hessen, 1991), 95.

2. Hans-Walter Schmuhl, "'Euthanasie' und Krankenmord," in Robert Jütte with Wolfgang Eckart, Hans-Walter Schmuhl, and Winfried Süss, *Medizin und Nationalsozialismus: Bilanz und Perspektiven der Forschung* (Göttingen: Wallstein Verlag, 2011), 214.

3. Henry Friedlander, *The Origins of Nazi Genocide: From Euthanasia to the Final Solution* (Chapel Hill: University of North Carolina Press, 1995), 52; Michael Burleigh, *Death and Deliverance: 'Euthanasia' in Germany, 1900–1945* (Cambridge, UK: Cambridge University Press, 1995), 277.

4. Karl Binding and Alfred Hoche, *Die Freigabe der Vernichtung lebensunwerten Lebens. Ihr Mass und Ihre Form* (Leipzig: Felix Meiner, 1920), 27–32.

5. Binding and Hoche, *Die Freigabe der Vernichtung lebensunwerten Lebens*, 49–51, 62.

6. Alfred Hoche, *Jahresringe: Innenansicht eines Menschenlebens* (Munich, 1935), 22.

7. Binding and Hoche, *Die Freigabe der Vernichtung lebensunwerten Lebens*, 51, 56.

8. Florian Bruns, *Medizinethik im Nationalsozialismus: Entwicklungen und Protagonisten in Berlin (1939–1945)* (Stuttgart: Franz Steiner Verlag, 2009), 14–16, passim.

9. For information about the pre-Nazi German eugenics movement, see Richard Weikart, *From Darwin to Hitler: Evolutionary Ethics, Eugenics, and Racism in Germany* (New York: Palgrave Macmillan, 2004).

10. For a more detailed discussion of Hitler's views on euthanasia and how this fit into his broader worldview, see Richard Weikart, *Hitler's Ethic: The Nazi Pursuit of Evolutionary Progress* (New York: Palgrave Macmillan, 2009), esp. 179–187.

11. Hitler, interview with George Sylvester Viereck, published in *The American Monthly* (October 1923), in *Hitler Sämtliche Aufzeichnungen, 1905–1924*, ed. Eberhard Jäckel (Stuttgart: Deutsche Verlags-Anstalt, 1980), 1025.

12. "Ein Kampf um Deutschlands Freiheit" (February 5, 1928), in *Hitler: Reden, Schriften, Anordnungen, Febraur 1925 bis Januar 1933*, 6 vols. (Munich: K. G. Saur, 1992–2003), vol. 2, part 2: 665.

13. *Hitler's Second Book: The Unpublished Sequel to* Mein Kampf, ed. Gerhard L. Weinberg (New York: Enigma Books, 2003), 21.

14. Hitler, "Appell an die deutsche Kraft" (August 4, 1929), in *Hitler: Reden, Schriften, Anordnungen*, 3: 348–349.

15. "German Law Authorizes Sterilization for Prevention of Hereditary Diseases," *History Unfolded*, accessed February 2024, https://newspapers.ushmm.org/events /german-law-authorizes-sterilization-for-prevention-of-hereditary-diseases. This site provides links to contemporaneous newspaper stories about the German law.

16. *Opfer der Vergangenheit*; see also Burleigh, *Death and Deliverance*, 189; a brief edited clip from this film can be viewed on YouTube.

17. See Richard Weikart, *Darwinian Racism: How Darwinism Influenced Hitler, Nazism, and White Nationalism* (Seattle: Discovery Institute Press, 2022), chap. 5 (entitled "Nazi Eugenics and Euthanasia").

18. Hans-Christian Petersen and Sönke Zankel, "Werner Catel—ein Protagonist der NS-'Kindereuthanasie' und seine Nachkriegskarriere," *Medizinhistorisches Journal* 38, no. 2 (2003), 143–45.

19. Ulf Schmidt, *Karl Brandt: The Nazi Doctor: Medicine and Power in the Third Reich* (London: Hambledon Continuum, 2007), chap. 1–2, quote at 43.

20. Ulf Schmidt, *Justice at Nuremberg: Leo Alexander and the Nazi Doctors' Trial* (Houndsmills, UK: Palgrave Macmillan, 2004), 242–243.

21. Bettina Winter, ed., *"Verlegt nach Hadamar": Die Geschichte einer NS-"Euthanasie"-Anstalt* (Kassel: Landeswolfahrtsverband Hessen, 1991), 69.

22. Alexander Rossino, *Hitler Strikes Poland: Blitzkrieg, Ideology, and Atrocity* (Lawrence, KS: University Press of Kansas, 2003), 234 and passim.

23. Friedlander, *The Origins of Nazi Genocide*, 136–137.

24. Friedlander, *The Origins of Nazi Genocide*, 137–140.

25. Friedlander, *The Origins of Nazi Genocide*, 78–80.

26. On deaf people and euthanasia in Nazi Germany, see Horst Biesold, *Crying Hands: Eugenics and Deaf People in Nazi Germany* (Washington, DC: Gallaudet University Press, 1999), chap. 9.

27. On characteristics of victims, see Friedlander, *The Origins of Nazi Genocide*, chap. 9.

28. Friedlander, *The Origins of Nazi Genocide*, 170–171, 184; quotes at 170–171.

29. Bettina Winter, "Die Geschichte der NS-'Euthanasie'-Anstalt Hadamar," in *Verlegt nach Hadamar: Die Geschichte einer NS-"Euthanasie"-Anstalt*, ed. Bettina Winter (Kassel: Landeswohlfahrtsverbandes Hessen, 1991), 97.

30. Burleigh, *Death and Deliverance*, 205–217.

31. Nathan Stoltzfus, *Hitler's Compromises: Coercion and Consensus in Nazi Germany* (New Haven, CT: Yale University Press, 2016), 181–187.

32. "Excerpt from Bishop von Galen's Sermon (October 3, 1941)," *German History in Documents and Images*, accessed May 2024, http://germanhistorydocs.ghi-dc.org/pdf/eng/English82_Galen.pdf.

33. Alfred Rosenberg Diary, *United States Holocaust Museum*, December 14, 1941, 625, at http://collections.ushmm.org/view/2001.62.14; accessed January 22, 2014; see also the entry for December 14, 1941, in *Die Tagebücher von Joseph Goebbels*, ed. Elke Fröhlich, part II: *Diktate 1941–1945*, vol. 2: *Oktober-Dezember 1941* (Munich K. G. Saur, 1996), 506.

34. Friedlander, *The Origins of Nazi Genocide*, 297–298.

35. For photographs and details of each physician and official tried, see "Doctors' Trial," *Wikipedia*, last modified February 13, 2024, https://en.wikipedia.org/wiki/Doctors'_Trial.

36. Friedlander, *The Origins of Nazi Genocide*, 44–46, 53.

37. Werner Catel, interview, "Aus Menschlichkeit töten?," *Der Spiegel* Nr. 8 (1964): 41ff.

6. SINCE 1960: EUROPE REOPENS DEATH'S DOOR

1. Michael Cook, "Another Speed Bump for Belgian Euthanasia," *BioEdge: Bioethics News from around the World*, February 8, 2013, http://www.bioedge.org/index.php/bioethics/bioethics_article/10388. See also Michael Cook, "Belgian Psychiatrist Deregistered over Abuse," *BioEdge*, November 8, 2014, https://bioedge.org/end-of-life-issues/belgian-psychiatrist-deregistered-over-abuse/.

2. Guenther Lewy, *Assisted Death in Europe and America: Four Regimes and Their Lessons* (Oxford, UK: Oxford University Press, 2011), 19; John Griffiths et al., *Euthanasia and Law in Europe* (Oxford, UK: Hart Publishing, 2008), 14.

3. Griffiths et al., *Euthanasia and Law in Europe*, 24.

4. Henk A. M. J. ten Have and Jos V. M. Welie, *Death and Medical Power: An Ethical Analysis of Dutch Euthanasia Practice* (Maidenhead, UK: Open University Press, 2005), 39–40.

5. Griffiths et al., *Euthanasia and Law in Europe*, 14.

6. Ten Have and Welie, *Death and Medical Power*, 6–9.

7. "About NVVE," *NVVE*, accessed February 2024, https://www.nvve.nl/about-nvve.

8. Lewy, *Assisted Death in Europe and America*, 20.

9. Griffiths et al., *Euthanasia and Law in Europe*, 76–77.

10. Griffiths et al., *Euthanasia and Law in Europe*, 30–31.

11. R. Cohen-Almagor, *Euthanasia in the Netherlands: The Policy and Practice of Mercy Killing* (Dordrecht: Springer-Kluwer, 2004), 49.

12. Griffiths et al., *Euthanasia and Law in Europe*, 154.

13. Johannes J. M. van Delden et al., "The Remmelink Study Two Years Later," *The Hastings Center Report* 23, no. 6 (1993): 24.

14. Griffiths et al., *Euthanasia and Law in Europe*, 71–72.

15. Lewy, Assisted Death in Europe and America, 33.

16. Griffiths et al., *Euthanasia and Law in Europe*, 114.

17. Lewy, *Assisted Death in Europe and America*, 26.

18. Lewy, *Assisted Death in Europe and America*, 29.

19. Antina de Jong and Gert van Dijk, "Euthanasia in the Netherlands: Balancing Autonomy and Compassion," *World Medical Journal* 63, no. 3 (October 2017): 11–12.

20. Regional Euthanasia Review Committees, Netherlands, *Annual Report 2019*, 8 and 10, accessed March 19, 2021, https://english.euthanasiecommissie.nl/the -committees/documents/publications/annual-reports/2002/annual-reports /annual-reports.

21. Jeanne Smits, "Dutch Court Acquits Man Who Euthanized His Mother after Doctor Refused," *LifeSite-News*, May 21, 2015, https://www.lifesitenews.com/opinion/ dutch-court-acquits-man-who-euthanized-his-mother-after-doctor-refused

22. "Doctor Cleared of Murder in Euthanasia Case Says She Would Do It Again," *Dutch News*, June 15, 2020, https://www.dutchnews.nl/news/2020/06/ doctor-cleared-of-murder-in-euthanasia-case-says-she-would-do-it-again/

23. Ten Have and Welie, *Death and Medical Power*, 2.

24. Kersten Evenblij et al., "Physicians' Experiences with Euthanasia: A Cross-Sectional Survey amongst a Random Sample of Dutch Physicians to Explore Their Concerns, Feelings, and Pressure," *BMC Family Practice* 20, no. 1 (December 17, 2019): 2–3.

25. Scott Y. H. Kim et al., "Euthanasia and Assisted Suicide of Patients with Psychiatric Disorders in the Netherlands 2011 to 2014," *JAMA Psychiatry* 73, no. 4 (2016): 362–368, https://jamanetwork.com/journals/jamapsychiatry/fullarticle/2491354.

26. "Careful and Caring," *Expertise Centrum Euthanasia*, 2019, https://expertisecentrumeuthanasie.nl/en/.

27. Regional Euthanasia Review Committees, Netherlands, *Annual Report 2019*, 15, accessed March 19, 2021, https://english.euthanasiecommissie.nl/the-committees /documents/publications/annual-reports/2002/annual-reports/annual-reports.

28. Regional Euthanasia Review Committees, Netherlands, *Annual Report 2019*, 12–13, 19; quotes at 8, 63, 47–48, accessed March 19, 2021, https://english .euthanasiecommissie.nl/the-committees/documents/publications/annual -reports/2002/annual-reports/annual-reports.

29. Griffiths et al., *Euthanasia and Law in Europe*, 276, 272, 305; Lewy, *Assisted Death in Europe and America*, 70.

30. Toni C. Saad, "Euthanasia in Belgium: Legal, Historical, and Political Review," *Issues in Law and Medicine* 32, no. 2 (Fall 2017): 189, quote at 192.

31. Kaspar Raus, et al., "Euthanasia in Belgium: Shortcomings of the Law and Its Application and the Monitoring of Practice," *Journal of Medicine and Philosophy* 46, no. 1 (2021): 92–93.

32. Michael Cook, "Not a Noble Death," *Mercatornet*, May 7, 2013, https://mercatornet.com/not_a_noble_death/14830/.

33. "Belgian Helped to Die after Three Sex Change Operations," *BBC News*, October 2, 2013, http://www.bbc.co.uk/news/world-europe-24373107.

34. Raus et al., "Euthanasia in Belgium," 88.

35. Saad, "Euthanasia in Belgium," 185.

36. Raus et al., "Euthanasia in Belgium," 102.

37. Raus et al., "Euthanasia in Belgium," 95.

38. Raus et al., "Euthanasia in Belgium," 93–95.

39. Raus et al., "Euthanasia in Belgium," 81–82, 89–91.

40. Griffiths et al., *Euthanasia and Law in Europe*, 472, 474–475.

41. Griffiths et al., *Euthanasia and Law in Europe*, 472.

42. Lewy, *Assisted Death in Europe and America*, 93, 98.

43. Sarah Vilpert et al., "Social, Cultural and Experiential Patterning of Attitudes and Behaviour towards Assisted Suicide in Switzerland: Evidence from a National Population-Based Study," *Swiss Medical Weekly* 150, no. 2526 (July 1, 2020), https://smw.ch/article/doi/smw.2020.20275.

44. Swiss government statistics, *Bundesamt für Statistik*, accessed May 2024, https://www.bfs.admin.ch/bfs/de/home/statistiken/gesundheit/gesundheitszustand /sterblichkeit-todesursachen/spezifische.assetdetail.7008105.html.

45. Vilpert et al., "Social, Cultural and Experiential Patterning of Attitudes and Behaviour."

46. "Review of the Year 2020 and Outlook for 2021," *Dignitas*, March 8, 2021, http://www.dignitas.ch/images/stories/pdf/medienmitteilung-08032021-e.pdf.

47. Griffiths et al., *Euthanasia and Law in Europe*, 473.

48. Lee Moran, "Italian Woman Pays $14G to Commit Suicide at Suicide Clinic Due to Being 'Sad about Losing Her Looks,'" *New York Daily News*, February 21, 2014, https://www.nydailynews.com/news/world/ italian-woman-pays-14g-commit-suicide-due-losing-article-1.1622200.

49. Joachim Cohen et al., "Public Acceptance of Euthanasia in Europe: A Survey Study in 47 Countries," *International Journal of Public Health* 59 (2014): 145–146.

50. Rahul Garg, "Austria Constitutional Court Strikes Down Ban on Assisted Death," *Jurist*, December 14, 2020, https://www.jurist.org/news/2020/12/austria -constitutional-court-strikes-down-ban-on-assisted-death.

51. John Griffiths et al., *Euthanasia and Law in Europe* (Oxford, UK: Hart Publishing, 2008), 369, 375.

52. Mattieu Goar, "Assisted Dying: Macron Moves to Depoliticize the Debate," *Le Monde*, accessed January 13, 2023, https://www.lemonde.fr/en/politics/article /2022/11/09/assisted-dying-french-president-emmanuel-macron-is-trying-to -depoliticize-the-debate_6003481_5.html.

53. Griffiths et al., *Euthanasia and Law in Europe*, 369, 375.

54. N. D. A. Kemp, *'Merciful Release': The History of the British Euthanasia Movement* (Manchester: Manchester University Press, 2002), 178, 191–192, 200, 210; quote at 225.

55. Udo Benzenhöfer, *Der gute Tod? Euthanasie und Sterbehilfe in Geschichte und Gegenwart* (Munich: C. H. Beck, 1999), 138–140.

56. "Germany's Top Court Paves the Way for Assisted Suicide," *Deutsche Welle*, February 26, 2020, https://www.dw.com/en/germanys-top-court-paves -the-way-for-assisted-suicide/a-52531371.

57. Andrew Coyne, "The Slippery Slope that Leads to Death," *Globe and Mail*, November 21, 1994.

7. The United States and Canada Today

1. Sean Boynton, "Trudeau Says Assisted Dying Offers to Veterans 'Unacceptable' as Cases Mount," *Global News*, December 2, 2022, https://globalnews.ca/news /9321582/veterans-affairs-maid-cases-trudeau/; accessed February 14, 2023.

2. "Humanist Manifesto II" [1973], *American Humanist Association*, accessed December 2013, http://www.americanhumanist.org/Humanism /Humanist_Manifesto_II.

3. Howard Ball, *At Liberty to Die: The Battle for Death with Dignity in America* (New York: New York University Press, 2012), 32–36.

4. Derek Humphry and Mary Clement, *Freedom to Die: People, Politics, and the Right-to-Die Movement* (New York: St. Martin's Press, 1998), 31, 95; Ian Dowbiggin, *A Merciful End: The Euthanasia Movement in Modern America* (Oxford, UK: Oxford University Press, 2003), 121.

5. Ball, *At Liberty to Die*, 37–46.

6. Dowbiggin, *A Merciful End*, xvi–xvii, 106–108, 118.

7. James Rachels, "Active and Passive Euthanasia," *New England Journal of Medicine* 292 (1975): 78–80. The article is available at https://rintintin.colorado.edu /~vancecd/phil1100/Rachels.pdf.

8. Faith Karimi, "Teens Who Laughed and Recorded a Drowning Man in His Final Moments Won't Face Charges," *CNN News*, June 26, 2018, https://www.cnn.com /2018/06/26/us/florida-teens-no-charges-drowning-man/index.html.

9. Dowbiggin, *A Merciful End*, 98.

10. Derek Humphrey, "The Case for Rational Suicide," in *Last Rights? Assisted Suicide and Euthanasia Debated*, ed. Michael M. Uhlmann (Washington, DC: Ethics and Public Policy Center, 1998), 308.

11. Humphry and Clement, *Freedom to Die*, 100–115.

12. Derek Humphry and Ann Wickett, *The Right to Die: Understanding Euthanasia* (New York: Harper and Row, 1986), 293–94; Humphry and Clement, *Freedom to Die*, 111.

13. Humphry and Clement, *Freedom to Die*, 5–6, 14.

14. Humphry and Clement, *Freedom to Die*, 49

15. Humphry and Clement, *Freedom to Die*, 6.

16. Humphry and Clement, *Freedom to Die*, 313.

17. Neal Nicol and Harry Wylie, *Between the Dying and the Dead: Dr. Jack Kevorkian's Life and the Battle to Legalize Euthanasia* (Madison: Terrace Books, University of Wisconsin Press, 2006), 1–2, 37, 66–67, 116.

18. Nicol and Wylie, *Between the Dying and the Dead*, 147, 187.

19. Nicol and Wylie, *Between the Dying and the Dead*, 21.

20. Joe Swickard, et al, "Jack Kevorkian Sparked a Debate on Death," *Detroit Free Press*, June 3, 2011, https://web.archive.org/web/20110915113206/http://www.freep.com/article/20110604/NEWS05/106040427; Rita Marker, *Deadly Compassion: The Death of Ann Humphry and the Truth about Euthanasia* (New York: William Morrow and Company, 1993), 166, 171–172.

21. For a good summary of the founding of bioethics, see Renée C. Fox and Judith P. Swazey, *Observing Bioethics* (Oxford, UK: Oxford University Press, 2008).

22. Peter Singer, *Writings on an Ethical Life* (New York: Ecco, 2000), 77–78, 220–221.

23. Peter Singer, *Practical Ethics* (Cambridge, UK: Cambridge University Press, 1979), 12–13.

24. Singer, *Practical Ethics*, chap. 7.

25. Peter Singer, "Rethinking Life and Death: A New Ethical Approach," in *Last Rights?*, 174, 179–180. For more on Singer, see Richard Weikart, *The Death of Humanity: And the Case for Life* (Washington, DC: Regnery Faith, 2016), 4–5, 52–53, 56–58, 177–181, 236–238.

26. Margaret Pabst Battin, *Ending Life: Ethics and the Way We Die* (Oxford, UK: Oxford University Press, 2005), 7–8, 20–21, 25–27, 39.

27. Paul Ramsey, *Ethics at the Edges of Life: Medical and Legal Intersections* (New Haven, CT: Yale University Press, 1978), 146–151.

28. American Medical Association, *Code of Medical Ethics*, chap. 5, accessed January 23, 2023, https://www.ama-assn.org/system/files/2019-06/code-of-medical-ethics-chapter-5.pdf.

29. "It's Over, Debbie," in *Last Rights?*, chap. 16.

30. Marker, *Deadly Compassion*, 83.

31. Timothy Quill, "Death and Dignity," in *Last Rights?*, chap. 17.

32. "The Oregon Death with Dignity Act (1998)," in *The Right to Die Debate: A Documentary History*, ed. Marjorie B. Zucker (Westport, CN: Greenwood Press, 1999), 274–281.

33. "The Oregon Death with Dignity Act (1998)," 274–281.

34. James Reinl, "America Is Racing Towards Canada's Euthanasia Free-For-All," *Daily Mail*, February 11, 2023, https://www.dailymail.co.uk/news/article -11711353/Seven-states-eye-legalizing-assisted-suicide-America.html.

35. "Oregon Death with Dignity Act: 2021 Data Summary," February 28, 2022, http://www.oregon.gov/oha/PH/PROVIDERPARTNERRESOURCES /EVALUATIONRESEARCH/DEATHWITHDIGNITYACT/Documents /year24.pdf.

36. Guenther Lewy, *Assisted Death in Europe and America: Four Regimes and Their Lessons* (Oxford, UK: Oxford University Press, 2011), 133.

37. "Oregon Death with Dignity Act: 2020 Data Summary," February 26, 2021, https://www.oregon.gov/oha/PH/PROVIDERPARTNERRESOURCES /EVALUATIONRESEARCH/DEATHWITHDIGNITYACT/Documents /year23.pdf

38. "Oregon Death with Dignity Act: 2021 Data Summary."

39. Neil Gorsuch, *The Future of Assisted Suicide and Euthanasia* (Princeton, NJ: Princeton University Press, 2006), chap. 2.

40. Ball, *At Liberty to Die*, 156–157.

41. John Paul II, "The Gospel of Life," in *Last Rights?*, chap. 10.

42. "Resolution on Assisted Suicide of the Southern Baptist Convention (June 1996)," in *The Right to Die Debate*, 262–263.

43. "Why Assisted Suicide Must Not Be Legalized," *Disability Rights Education and Defense Fund*, accessed February 6, 2023, https://dredf.org/public-policy /assisted-suicide/why-assisted-suicide-must-not-be-legalized/.

44. Gorsuch, *The Future of Assisted Suicide and Euthanasia*, 4–5.

45. Debbie Selby, Sally Bean, and Amy Nolen, "Medical Assistance in Dying (MAiD): A Descriptive Study from a Canadian Tertiary Care Hospital," *American Journal of Hospice and Palliative Medicine* 37, no. 1 (2019), https://journals.sage pub.com/doi/full/10.1177/1049909119859844.

46. "Third Annual Report on Medical Assistance in Dying in Canada 2021," Government of Canada, accessed February 8, 2023, https://www.canada.ca/en/health -canada/services/medical-assistance-dying/annual-report-2021.html.

47. "Canada's Medical Assistance in Dying (MAID) Law," Government of Canada, last accessed March 4, 2024, https://www.justice.gc.ca/eng/cj-jp/ad-am/bk-di .html.

48. "Third Annual Report on Medical Assistance in Dying in Canada 2021."

49. Cynthia Mulligan and Meredith Bond, "Ontario Man Applying for Medically-Assisted Death as Alternative to Being Homeless," *Toronto City News*, October 13, 2022, https://toronto.citynews.ca/2022/10/13/ medical-assistance-death-maid-canada/.

50. Samantha Kamman, "Homeless Man Seeks to End Life through Canada's Assisted Suicide Program," *Christian Post*, February 2, 2023, https://www.christianpost. com/news/homeless-man-seeks-assisted-suicide-death-citing-hopelessness.html; accessed February 14, 2023.

8. Euthanasia's End Game

1. Michelle Gamage, "She Sought Help in a Crisis and Was Suggested MAID Instead," *The Tyee*, August 9, 2023, https://thetyee.ca/News/2023/08/09 /Medical-Assistance-Dying-Slippery-Slope-Mental-Illness-Disabled/.

2. John Keown, *Euthanasia, Ethics, and Public Policy: An Argument against Legalisation* (Cambridge, UK: Cambridge University Press, 2002).

3. Mark Komrad, "Assisted Suicide or Assisted Dying: A Debate," *American Psychiatric Association Conference*, San Francisco, May 20, 2019.

4. Margaret Pabst Battin, *Ending Life: Ethics and the Way We Die* (Oxford, UK: Oxford University Press, 2005), 25–27, 39.

5. "Is Human Life Intrinsically Valuable?" radio debate between Richard Weikart, Peter Singer, and Susan Blackmore, *Unbelievable with Justin Brierley*, 2016, Premier Christian Radio, https://www.premier.plus/unbelievable/podcasts/episodes/classic -replay-is-human-life-intrinsically-valuable-peter-singer-richard-weikart-amp -susan-blackmore.

6. Peter Singer, *Practical Ethics* (Cambridge, UK: Cambridge University Press, 1979), 84, 122–125.

7. David Lamb, *Down the Slippery Slope: Arguing in Applied Ethics* (London: Croom Helm, 1988), 120.

8. Irene Tuffrey-Wijne, et al., "Euthanasia and Physician-Assisted Suicide in People with Intellectual Disabilities and/or Autism Spectrum Disorders: Investigation of 39 Dutch Case Reports (2012–2021)," *BJPsych Open* (May 23, 2023), https://www.cambridge.org/core/journals/bjpsych-open/article/euthanasia-and -physicianassisted-suicide-in-people-with-intellectual-disabilities-andor-autism -spectrum-disorders-investigation-of-39-dutch-case-reports-20122021/93B38EA E616E0A6C378BE308C87253A2#article. Despite the stipulation in the Dutch and Belgian euthanasia laws that the patient has to be enduring unbearable suffering, this does not mean that they need be in excruciating pain. Moreover, surveys given to patients electing assisted suicide indicate that most of them do not choose assisted suicide because they are suffering from pain. Indeed, many patients opting for euthanasia in these two countries are not in pain at all. In a 1990 survey of patients requesting euthanasia in the Netherlands, only 46 percent indicated that pain was a significant factor causing them to choose euthanasia. However, 57 percent indicated that loss of dignity was a reason, and 23 percent listed tiredness of life as a factor. See Guenther Lewy, *Assisted Death in Europe and America: Four Regimes and Their Lessons* (Oxford University Press, 2011), 32–33.

9. Gregory Pike, "Euthanasia and Assisted Suicide—When Choice Is an Illusion and Informed Consent Fails," *Bios Centre*, accessed May 2024, https://bioscentre.org /articles/euthanasia-and-assisted-suicide-when-choice-is-an-illusion-and -informed-consent-fails/.

10. Keown, *Euthanasia, Ethics, and Public Policy*, 108–110.

11. Yonette Joseph and Iliana Magra, "David Goodall, 104, Scientist Who Fought to Die on His Own Terms, Ends His Life," *New York Times*, May 10, 2018, https://www.nytimes.com/2018/05/10/world/europe/david-goodall-australia -scientist-dead.html.

12. Jeremy Gahagan, "Genevieve Lhermitte: Belgian Mother Who Killed Her Five Children Euthanised," *BBC News*, March 3, 2023, https://www.bbc.com/news/world-europe-64835051.

13. Michael Cook, "Euthanasia Is Now Being Performed... on Prisoners," *Intellectual Takeout*, March 6, 2018, https://intellectualtakeout.org/2018/03/euthanasia-is-now-being-performed-on-prisoners/.

14. Michael Cook, "Is the Death Penalty Sneaking Back Disguised as Euthanasia in Belgium?," *Mercator*, March 10, 2023, https://www.mercatornet.com/is-the-death-penalty-sneaking-back-disguised-as-euthanasia-in-belgium/

15. Keown, *Euthanasia, Ethics, and Public Policy*, 76.

16. Alex Schadenberg, "Canadian Man Claims that He Was Pressured to Request Euthanasia," *Euthanasia Prevention Coalition*, November 10, 2022, https://alexschadenberg.blogspot.com/2022/11/canadian-man-claims-that-assisted-death.html.

17. Quoted in Lamb, *Down the Slippery Slope*, 93.

18. Matthew Parris, "Ignore the Reactionaries Who Oppose Assisted Dying," *Spectator*, February 3, 2024, https://www.spectator.co.uk/article/ignore-the-reactionaries-who-oppose-assisted-dying/.

19. Janet Lyon, "On the Asylum Road with Woolf and Mew," *Modernism* 18, no. 3 (2012): 558.

20. Keown, *Euthanasia, Ethics, and Public Policy*, 78–79.

21. Neil Gorsuch, *The Future of Assisted Suicide and Euthanasia* (Princeton University Press, 2006), 108, 115.

22. Michael Cook, "Belgian Surgeons Welcome Euthanasia Organs," *Mercator*, June 17, 2011, https://www.mercatornet.com/belgian_surgeons_welcome_euthanasia_organs.

23. Amanda Pfeffer, "Ontario Doctors Challenge Policy Forcing Referrals for Medically Assisted Dying," *CBC News*, June 15, 2017, https://www.cbc.ca/news/canada/ottawa/medically-assisted-dying-ontario-college-1.4159660. See also Travis Carpenter and Lucas Vivas, "Ethical Arguments against Coercing Provider Participation in MaiD (medical assistance in dying) in Ontario, Canada," *BMC Medical Ethics*, June 3, 2020, https://www.ncbi.nlm.nih.gov/pmc/articles/PMC7271423/.

9. Doing As I Please

1. "Oregon Woman Who Asked for Assisted Suicide Is Alive Because Her Doctor Helped Her Find Something to Live for," *Euthanasia Prevention Coalition*, November 19, 2018, https://alexschadenberg.blogspot.com/2018/11/oregon-woman-decided-not-to-die-by.html?utm_source=Euthanasia+Prevention+Coalition+Contacts&utm_campaign=0a1fb76fb3-EMAIL_CAMPAIGN_2018_11_23_04_58_COPY_03&utm_medium=email&utm_term=0_105a5cdd2d-0a1fb76fb3-198481989.

2. Margaret Pabst Battin, *Ending Life: Ethics and the Way We Die* (Oxford, UK: Oxford University Press, 2005), 20.

3. Jonathan Pugh, *Autonomy, Rationality, and Contemporary Bioethics* (Oxford, UK: Oxford University Press, 2020), https://www.ncbi.nlm.nih.gov/books/NBK556857/.

4. Ole Hartling, "We Need to Rethink the Idea of 'Dying with Dignity,'" *Mercator*, November 29, 2021, https://www.mercatornet.com/we-need-to-rethink -the-idea-of-dying-with-dignity.

5. Ronald W. Pies and Cynthia M. A. Geppert, "Physician-Assisted Suicide and the Autonomy Myth," *Psychiatric Times* (October 27, 2021), https://www .psychiatrictimes.com/view/physician-assisted-suicide-and-the-autonomy-myth.

6. Henk A. M. J. ten Have and Jos V. M. Welie, *Death and Medical Power: An Ethical Analysis of Dutch Euthanasia Practice* (Maidenhead, England: Open University Press, 2005), 16.

7. Ten Have and Welie, *Death and Medical Power*, 2–6.

8. Neil Gorsuch, *The Future of Assisted Suicide and Euthanasia* (Princeton, NJ: Princeton UP, 2006), 123.

9. Gregory K. Pike, "Euthanasia and Assisted Suicide—When Choice Is an Illusion and Informed Consent Fails," *Bios Centre*, accessed May 2024, https://bioscentre .org/articles/euthanasia-and-assisted-suicide-when-choice-is-an-illusion-and -informed-consent-fails/#_ftn280.

10. Alexander Raikin, "No Other Options," *The New Atlantis*, December 16, 2022, https://www.thenewatlantis.com/publications/no-other-options.

11. Alexander Raikin, "No Other Options."

12. "Ontario Man Asks for MAiD Based on Long Term Care Access," *Euthanasia Prevention Coalition*, December 9, 2022, https://alexschadenberg.blogspot.com /2022/12/ontario-man-asks-for-maid-based-on-long.html.

13. Alexander Raikin, "No Other Options."

14. Alexander Raikin, "No Other Options."

15. Pies and Geppert, "Physician-Assisted Suicide and the Autonomy Myth."

16. Pies and Geppert, "Physician-Assisted Suicide and the Autonomy Myth."

17. Alexander Raikin, "No Other Options."

18. L. Ganzini et al., "Physician's Experiences with the Oregon Death with Dignity Act," *New England Journal of Medicine* 342, no. 8 (February 24, 2000): 557–563, https://pubmed.ncbi.nlm.nih.gov/10684915/.

19. See, for instance, Ole Hartling, *Euthanasia and the Ethics of a Doctor's Decisions: An Argument against Assisted Dying*, trans. Tim Davies (London: Bloomsbury Academic, 2021).

20. Hartling, "We Need to Rethink the Idea of 'Dying with Dignity.'"

21. Claire Williams, "Assisted Suicide: 'I Was Devastated by My Husband's Assisted Death,'" *BBC News*, November 22, 2018, https://www.bbc.com/news /uk-46281929.

22. Hannah Roberts, "Italian Woman, 85, Ends Her Life at Swiss Euthanasia Clinic Because She Was Upset about Losing Her Looks," *Daily Mail*, February 20, 2014, https://www.dailymail.co.uk/news/article-2564023/Italian-woman-85-ends-life -Swiss-Dignitas-clinic-upset-losing-looks.html.

23. Richard Weikart, *Made in the Image of God: Why Human Dignity Argues for a Creator* (Lafayette, IN: Ratio Christi Press, 2022), https://press.ratiochristi.org/product/are-you-the-image-of-god/.

Conclusion: Redefining Death with Dignity

1. Luke 14:12–14.
2. "Third Annual Report on Medical Assistance in Dying in Canada 2021," *Government of Canada*, accessed February 2024, https://www.canada.ca/en/health-canada/services/medical-assistance-dying/annual-report-2021.html.
3. Alexander Raikin, "No Other Options," *New Atlantis*, December 16, 2022, https://www.thenewatlantis.com/publications/no-other-options.
4. Vivek H. Murthy, "Our Epidemic of Loneliness and Isolation: US Surgeon General's Advisory on the Healing Effects of Social Connection and Community," *US Department of Health and Human Services*, 2023, https://www.hhs.gov/sites/default/files/surgeon-general-social-connection-advisory.pdf.

Acknowledgments

Scholarship is always a joint enterprise, and I thank all the scholars who have contributed to our knowledge of this subject. Their names are found in my endnotes. I especially want to thank those who read the manuscript and helped me improve it: Ian Dowbiggin, Nancy Pearcey, and Scott Rae. Amanda Witt, Jonathan Witt, and others at Discovery Institute Press have gone above and beyond the call of duty to improve my book. Many thanks.

INDEX

Made in United States
Troutdale, OR
08/06/2024